CHASING THE MODERN

"In this absorbing, elegant biography of his grandfather, Tony Hsu has given us much more than the story of one of China's most important early twentieth-century poets; he has also opened a rare window into the ways in which art and literature led China out of feudalism and into the modern world. As Xu Zhimo's poetry pushed past the boundaries of his era, so did his struggle to live and love as a modern man—giving this book a level of novelistic power not often found in even the most rewarding works of history."

—NICOLE MONES,
author of *Night in Shanghai* and *The Last Chinese Chef*

"In *Chasing the Modern*, Tony Hsu has gifted us with a graceful and yet unsparing peephole into the life of Xu Zhimo, whose pristine poetry was drawn from an unexpectedly short and turbulent life. This is the best sort of biography; one with all the drive, tension, and unflinching honesty of a first-rate historical novel. That Xu's story happens to be true makes it all the more remarkable."

—JENNIFER CODY EPSTEIN,
author of *The Gods of Heavenly Punishment*

"A captivating page-turner that sheds light on the intimate thoughts and tumultuous life of Xu Zhimo, one of China's most important twentieth-century poets. In Tony Hsu's exploration of his grandfather's life, we see the backdrop of China's momentous march toward modernity come to life—as well as a vivid portrait of a man who lived, loved, and wrote memorably."

—CHERYL LU-LIEN TAN,
author of *Sarong Party Girls* and *A Tiger in the Kitchen*

"The richness and beauty of Xu Zhimo's poems are deepened for us by this new biography by Tony Hsu. In a labor of love, Hsu has visited the sites of the poet's travels and sojourns and amassed an imposing amount of information from biographies, diaries, letters, memoirs and interviews. In addition to the nuanced portrait of Zhimo himself, his grandson treats with sympathetic understanding the three women who shared in the poet's search for love."

—CYRIL BIRCH,
professor emeritus at UC Berkeley

"It is the moment to commemorate all the milestones of great Chinese poetry in the twentieth century so as to raise our awareness of how meaningful the role of poetry is in the new era of globalization. With this aim in mind, Xu Zhimo and Tony Hsu prove the continuity of Chinese poetry, or simply, poetry, to us. *Chasing the Modern* is wonderful and substantial."

—YANG LIAN,
poet and author of *Where the Sea Stands Still*

"*Chasing the Modern* offers extraordinary insights into the life of a genius—one whose far too brief existence in this world was marked by both an infectious *joie de vivre* and a dark tragedy, qualities reflected in his timeless poems. In turn, Tony Hsu has drawn a complex portrait of this tormented legendary Chinese poet. A brilliant tribute!"

—BEN WANG,
co-chair of the Renwen Society, New York

"A gorgeously written tribute to one of the most acclaimed poets in modern Chinese history and his impact on the culture of the day. Tony Hsu's connection with his illustrious grandfather comes alive in these pages, as he tells of the complex and sometimes tragic life of Xu Zhimo, a life that yielded a wealth of evocative poetry. *Chasing the Modern* will make you want to track it down, and read it."

—KAVITA DASWANI,
author of *For Matrimonial Purposes*

CHASING
THE MODERN

The Twentieth-Century

Life of Poet

XU ZHIMO

TONY S. HSU

CAM RIVERS
PUBLISHING

CONTENTS

To my courageous and compassionate
grandmother Zhang Youyi and
my loving parents, Xu Jikai and Zhang Cuiwen,
through whom our family stories lived on.

Zhang Youyi, Xu Zhimo's first wife and the
author's grandmother, poses with her son
Xu Jikai in Shanghai, mid-1930s.

The author's parents, Xu Jikai and
Zhang Cuiwen, in the U.S., late 1940s.

For the most part, I used pinyin, a system of transliterating Chinese into the Latin alphabet, for names, places, and events throughout this book, except in the case of certain entities such as Peking University, which continues to refer to itself by the Wade-Giles system, an older mode of transliteration.

Xu Zhimo had three major women in his life, Zhang Youyi, Lin Huiyin, and Lu Xiaoman, and I refer to them by their first names, which to me felt more appropriate and more effectively established their identities.

Names and terms that appear in bold type throughout the book are defined and explained in the Glossary section. People whose names appear in bold italicized type are featured in short biographies.

I am immensely grateful to the many professors, academics, and writers whose research and translations I relied on to write this book. I have acknowledged my sources in the section "Works Cited and Consulted" and have included translation credits in the section "Translation Credits."

XU ZHIMO'S AWAKENING: HOW CAMBRIDGE IGNITED THE POET WITHIN

I t is a pleasure and an honor to write a brief foreword to this book by Tony Hsu about his grandfather, the Chinese poet and writer Xu Zhimo. I met Tony in August 2012 in my capacity as "keeper" of the memorial stone commemorating Xu's life, which stands by the bridge in King's College, Cambridge, where Xu studied for two years. We have since explored Xu's world together, culminating in this book as well as the 2014 exhibition *Xu Zhimo, Cambridge and China* in collaboration with Xu's home city of Haining, which was held in the great chapel in King's College.

This is the perfect moment for such a book. Xu's life and work were central to the first great opening up of China to Western artistic and literary influences during the quarter century after the establishment of the Republic of China in 1911. During that period, the country, which had been largely separated from the West, witnessed an incoming flood of philosophical, educational, aesthetic, scientific, literary, and scholarly ideas from the West, not dissimilar in force to the great tidal waves that occur seasonally near Haining.

Now, with the restoration of China as a world leader in economic and political terms, China is again eagerly embracing all the civilized arts of the West and fusing them with her ancient traditions. It is a moment like the 1920s, when there was an enormous outward curiosity and engagement.

The tide flows equally in the other direction, however. Xu Zhimo and several other distinguished Chinese thinkers who were his friends—Liang Qichao and Wang Guowei among them—deeply influenced the West. They invited a number of scholars to China, not only Cambridge figures like Goldsworthy Lowes Dickinson but other great thinkers, such as Rabindranath Tagore from India, who became a personal friend of Xu's. Several King's College intellectuals and artists—Arthur Waley with his translations of the great Chinese and Japanese classics, Roger Fry with his lectures introducing Chinese art to academic audiences in the West, Lowes Dickinson with his various writings—all brought

Xu in a Chinese silk gown. The poet's life and work were central to the first great opening up of China to Western artistic and literary influences in the early 1900s.

Chinese civilization westward. The same two-way rush is happening today. Not only is China becoming Western, but the West is becoming heavily influenced by the Chinese.

The force of Xu's impact was the result of several intersecting pieces of good fortune, which set the context for his brilliant mind and personality. They crystallized in the two years he spent at King's College from 1921 to 1922. Cambridge at that time was just recovering from the horrors of World War I. It was filled with great scientists, anthropologists, philosophers, and writers. In particular, there was the Bloomsbury Group with its joint attachments to London and King's College. Over the years its members included the economist John Maynard Keynes, the writers Virginia Woolf and E. M. Forster, and the artists Duncan Grant and Roger Fry. Several Bloomsbury Group intellectuals became Xu's close friends and mentors.

King's College was particularly congenial and stimulating as a setting, for it had recently been the college of one of the last great romantic poets, Rupert Brooke, and of the writer of ghostly tales of the weird, M. R. James (who left his provostship two years before Xu arrived). It was a college that saw its role in education as extending far beyond straight academic work. Its great chapel emphasized music, poetry, literature, art, and, above all, conversation in the various clubs and informal meetings, including the secret society of the Apostles.

So Xu, with his charm and curiosity, mingled with an intellectual and artistic elite, not only in Cambridge but across all of England, where his friends and contacts included Bertrand Russell, Thomas Hardy, H. G. Wells, Katherine Mansfield, John Middleton Murry, I. A. Richards, Joseph Conrad, and Robert Bridges.

Xu found Cambridge as stimulating to his senses as it was to his mind. This point is particularly important in the making of a great poet, as it had been to the succession of poets who had come to Cambridge before him, including Marlowe, Milton, Donne, Marvell, Dryden, Wordsworth, Coleridge, Byron, and Tennyson, whose work Xu discovered there for the first time. The beauty of the willow-banked River Cam evoked, as his writing shows, memories of his home in China from which he had been so long absent. The wonders of the great lawns and extraordinarily well preserved architecture must have lifted his spirit and been the perfect setting for his conversion to poetry.

To ignite the intellectual and sensual, one final ingredient was required: his first passionate love affair, as described in this book.

It was indeed a heady mixture: new ideas; the deep friendship of a number of older men schooled in the Old Etonian–King's College tradition of counting deep friendship as one of the great arts of life; the beauties of nature crafted by art; the sudden encounter with the romantic poets, whose poetry had long been largely unknown in China.

Xu incorporated all of these elements into his most famous poem, "A Second Farewell to Cambridge," written after his third visit to Cambridge. In this poem he fused two ancient and remarkable places, the China he knew, descended from its great days when the southern Song city of Hangzhou had entranced Marco Polo and been the greatest city in the world, and Cambridge, a university over seven hundred years old when he first visited it, the home to more beauty and interesting ideas than almost anywhere else on earth.

Xu's passion for Cambridge also recast the way the British saw their own country; he showed them that it did not consist solely of overpopulated commercial centers. He was the first Chinese to write with great feeling about British architecture and landscape, and that, in turn, inspired the British to see their country with new eyes again.

As China and the West again merge, Xu Zhimo stands as a symbol of mutual curiosity and the desire to fuse the best of these two contrasting worlds. His fascinating life, as told by Tony Hsu, is a fitting tribute to the remarkable effects of intercultural understanding that have taken place again and again in world history, but nowhere more dramatically than in this single life of a great man and poet.

Alan Macfarlane
Professor Emeritus, King's College, Cambridge

Xu Zhimo's original chop and signature.

I am a cloud in the sky,
By chance casting a shadow on the ripples of your heart.
　　No need to be surprised,
　　Even less to rejoice—
The shadow vanishes in a wink.

You and I met on the sea at night;
You had your direction, I had mine.
　　You may remember,
　　Better yet forget—
The light emitted at the moment of encounter.

　　—Xu Zhimo, May 1926

I t has been said that human beings have an instinctual drive to seek out their ancestors, to see which physical features they share, to sense the timbre of their voices, to understand how they lived their lives, to know where their particular geniuses and profound flaws lay. If evolutionary science tells us anything, it is that their intelligence and experience are lodged in our DNA, and their disposition and mental and physical gifts influence our own. To know one's ancestors is to know oneself, and this inherent drive to know my own ancestors in part informed the curiosity I have always had about my grandfather Xu Zhimo.

As a child of an immigrant family from Shanghai growing up in a modest house in Queens, New York, I often passed the framed photograph of my grandfather from the 1920s in our dining room. He was dressed in a silk Mandarin-collared jacket and round spectacles, a definite contrast to the T-shirt and jeans I wore every day. His work—as a poet and an intellectual—was so different from my father's job as an engineer and my after-school boyhood job delivering newspapers. Sometimes I paused and imagined the man in the photograph speaking to me.

It wasn't until I was an engineering student—one of the few of Chinese descent—at the University of Michigan that I realized the extent of my grandfather's legacy. A college friend had picked up a flyer announcing that the UC Berkeley Chinese literature professor Cyril Birch had recently lectured on campus about Xu Zhimo's intellectual relationship with Thomas Hardy. Seeing that the Chinese last name matched my own, my friend handed me the flyer as a joke, asking, "Hey, is he a relative of yours?" That small facetious gesture set me on an odyssey to discover who this Chinese poet, my grandfather, was.

This search has taken me to eight countries on three continents and one subcontinent, where I spoke to academics, authors, family members and acquaintances, and the descendants of Xu Zhimo's friends. I have pored over numerous theses, articles, and books written about the poet. I have been fortunate enough to have had lengthy conversations with such Xu Zhimo scholars as Dr. Gaylord Leung, Professor Leo Ou-fan Lee of Harvard University, Professor Cyril Birch of UC Berkeley, and Professor Michelle Yeh of UC Davis. The reporting and writing of this biography has led me down many different paths—to the Cambridge office of the renowned social scientist and philosopher Goldsworthy

Xu in Lu Shan, Jiangxi Province.

Lowes Dickinson and up to the rooftops of the King's College Chapel with Professor Emeritus Alan Macfarlane. I've peered through the clouded windows of the small, worn cottage in Sawston, England, where Xu Zhimo and his first wife, my grandmother Zhang Youyi, lived for a few difficult and unhappy months. I've had chai near the Susima tea club in Santiniketan that Rabindranath Tagore, the Indian poet and Asia's first Nobel Laureate, named after my grandfather. And I've climbed to the foothills in China where Xu met his end in 1931 in a small mail plane that carried him with two pilots of the Chinese National Aviation Corporation as it slammed into the hilly expanses near Mount Tai, instantly killing all three passengers.

Xu Zhimo lived in one of the most tumultuous and dynamic periods in China's history, and perhaps even in the world's. During the early twentieth century, the Chinese were decidedly looking outward, beyond their expansive borders, and questioning their position as the Middle Kingdom. The elite of the country were actively exploring the social mores, structures, and perspectives of the West, contemplating the integration of foreign ideas into their own culture. During his relatively short life, Xu Zhimo saw China abolish the imperial system and transform into a nation ruled by a modern-day president. The poet also witnessed his country's violent struggle as it searched for its place in the world against the backdrop of the Kuomintang and Mao Zedong's Chinese Communist Party fighting for national control.

During my years of research, I discovered many things that confirmed for me Xu Zhimo's gifts as a writer and social pioneer. I also came across many things that surprised and saddened me about his character and the choices he made, choices that affected—and, in some situations, deeply disappointed—the people with whom he was closest. Ultimately, I endeavored in these pages to paint a nuanced portrait of a man who, in his own way, changed the course of Chinese literature and society. He was a man who made progressive and sometimes flawed decisions that in turn influenced his country. His work as a poet captures his passion, his multi-faceted personality, and his conflicted perspectives. If I had to sum up my grandfather's life in a few words, I would say that he was a man who was as complex as the era in which he lived.

May this biography bring you greater insight into this modern Chinese poet, as well as a deeper understanding of China's history and traditions and how they have changed. Perhaps you will be inspired to pick up other translated works of Xu Zhimo and enjoy his poems, as so many Chinese readers have throughout the past century.

Tony S. Hsu
California, USA

CHAPTER ONE

CHASING THE MODERN

QUIETLY I AM LEAVING

JUST AS QUIETLY I CAME;

I SHAKE MY SLEEVES,

NOT TO BRING AWAY A PATCH OF CLOUD.

—FROM "A SECOND FAREWELL TO CAMBRIDGE," 1928

Today you can read these lines inscribed on a piece of white marble beside the River Cam at the end of the King's Bridge in Cambridge, England. The stone is a memorial to a man who had walked and contemplated nature and man's place in it in this serene setting, with its grand willow trees and ever-shifting clouds reflected in the quiet streams. The memorial turns out to be a fitting metaphor: During the decades since Xu Zhimo's death in 1931, the importance of his poetry has proven to be as enduring as the stone on which his words are now displayed.

Xu in 1918, age twenty-one, prior to leaving for the
United States to study at Clark College.

If you mention Xu's name in the West today, few people other than world literature professors and poetry enthusiasts might nod their heads in recognition. But in China, almost a century after his death, Xu has once again become one of the most popular poets. His work is now studied in schools and universities throughout the country. His face remains an iconic image, and a number of literary critics have likened him to John Keats, for his sensuous writing, and Percy Bysshe Shelley, for the ardor of his sentiments. Professor Leo Ou-fan Lee compared Xu to F. Scott Fitzgerald, citing how both writers won "immediate success" and were "more interested in life than art, each the spokesman and symbol of his own restless generation." Furthering the comparison, Lee added that Fitzgerald and Xu were "involved in similar courtships"—Fitzgerald with his high-born wife Zelda, a writer and artist who was diagnosed as schizophrenic and languished in a sanatorium, and Xu with his second wife, **Lu Xiaoman**, a renowned amateur Chinese opera singer, ballroom dancer, artist, socialite, and writer, who, like Zelda, spiraled into an illness that destroyed her marriage. In the case of Xiaoman, it was a devastating opium addiction.

Xu Zhimo has also been called the Chinese Ernest Hemingway, a reputation he earned for his international travels and writings in the first half of the twentieth century, and for the public scrutiny of his tumultuous romantic life. Like his American counterpart, Xu was a man who took the literature of the moment and marched it forward into modernity.

In many ways, Xu's identity and pivotal choices reflect a radically shifting China, one that was looking inward, examining its often stifling cultural traditions and political structures, as well as looking outward, accepting and integrating Western ideas into its rich, complex society. Xu both embraced his Chinese heritage and, at the same time, found himself captivated by the world beyond his native borders. He was deeply engaged with the intellectually stimulating life of Cambridge University, the English writers, philosophers, artists, and poets of the **Bloomsbury Group**, and the verdant beauty of England itself. He traveled through America, Europe, and Russia (on the Trans-Siberian Railway) and visited India and Japan. In each of these host countries he offered his ideas and vibrancy and in turn was deeply influenced by the intellectuals and artists he met there.

During his thirty-five years of life, Xu Zhimo wrote, lectured, collaborated, and dreamed fully. His life is both a celebration and a tragedy.

CHAPTER TWO

EARLY LIFE
IN CHINA

1897–1918

A SCHOLARLY CHILDHOOD

Xu Zhimo, also known as Hsu Chih-mo (the Wade-Giles romanization of his name), was born in Xiashi, a city near Hangzhou in Zhejiang Province, on January 15, 1897. His father was Xu Shenru, a thriving merchant and banker, and his mother was Qian Muying, the eldest daughter of a well-known scholar. Xu's father had high ambitions for his son to take over his hugely successful businesses. Involved in banking, silk and cotton milling, and soy sauce production, Xu Shenru fully supported his son's education, but it is not known if he ever expressed any desire for his son to pursue the arts.

During Xu's early boyhood, from ages three to ten, his parents provided private tutoring for him, their only child. Throughout this time the nation's political climate was in constant flux. The 1911 Revolution brought about the **fall of the Qing dynasty**, the last imperial dynasty of China. The upheaval was brutal, resulting in the deaths of some 2.5 million people. Thanks in part to their wealth and status, the Xu family emerged from the revolution unscathed.

Xu as a teenager in Xiashi, his hometown. The youth, voted class president of Hangzhou Middle School, was admired for his high level of intelligence and charisma.

In fact, Xu's father had supported the uprising in Hangzhou by supplying guns for the revolutionary soldiers. Safe within the rarefied confines of his family's graceful tiled-roof estate with its many courtyards, Xu enjoyed a happy and peaceful childhood.

By the time Xu was ten, he had impressed his teachers with his academic abilities. Many considered him a prodigy. By age twelve, he had gained a command of the Classical Chinese language, an intellectual feat comparable to reading Shakespearean literature. Continuing at the Prefectural Middle School in Hangzhou, the equivalent of a Western high school, Xu took courses in English, physics, chemistry, and geography. He was admired for his high level of intelligence and charisma and was voted class president. To family members, it looked likely that Xu would fulfill his father's expectations of succeeding him as the head of the family empire. There was one problem, however. Since childhood, Xu showed an abiding passion for literature, which took an unshakable hold on him.

ARRANGED MARRIAGE TO ZHANG YOUYI

In 1915 Xu continued his studies at a preparatory program at Peking University. But soon after beginning his coursework he had to return home to Xiashi. His parents had arranged a marriage for him, a common occurrence for young men of his status. Xu, then eighteen, was to marry **Zhang Youyi**, fifteen. Their match had first been considered a few years prior to their wedding, when both were in their early teens.

The story of how Xu came to the attention of the influential Zhang family is a fitting one. Youyi's fourth-oldest brother, **Zhang Jiaao**, a high-ranking official of the Zhejiang military authority, had read Xu's academic composition "On the Relationship Between Fiction and Society." The work impressed Jiaao with its level of thought, use of **Classical and vernacular Chinese**, and extraordinary calligraphy. Jiaao then suggested the match to Xu's parents, and both families eagerly agreed.

However, when a matchmaker checked the pair's compatibility by consulting the Chinese calendar, she discovered the bride was born during a year incom-

Xu and Youyi, shortly after she journeyed from China to France in 1921. Three years in the West alone had radically changed Xu. He would ask Youyi for a divorce less than a year later.

patible with Xu's—under the inappropriate sign of the rat. The fortune-teller told the Zhangs that they could rectify the situation by altering the record of their daughter's birth year. They changed it from 1900 to 1898 so that she would seem to be born harmoniously in the year of the dog, according to the Chinese zodiac. Ultimately, this attempt to alter fate would bring disastrous results.

Xu's union with his new bride began on a promising note: Youyi was educated, well mannered, and progressive in outlook. Her brothers were accomplished, learned, and well respected. Jiaao, who had suggested the match, was a lauded and innovative Shanghai banker and would later become the president of the Bank of China. Youyi's second-oldest brother, **Zhang Junmai**, was an intellectual involved in politics who counted the famous writer and scholar *Liang Qichao* as part of his inner circle.

Of course, Xu and Youyi's true compatibility could not be measured before the marriage. As Chinese tradition dictated, the betrothed could not meet each other before their wedding day. Nonetheless, Youyi was well aware of her husband-to-be's interest in modernity. She showed her respect for his progressive leanings in her choice of wedding dress. While Western gowns are white, traditional Chinese gowns are red. Youyi chose to wear pink, a melding of Eastern and Western customs.

Despite the early promise, the match turned out to be a less than propitious one. The newlyweds moved into the Xiashi family home with Xu's parents, as was customary, but Youyi told her biographer decades later that her husband did not warm to her and never expressed an interest in communicating with her. A few years into their marriage, Youyi heard from a family servant how the sixteen-year-old Xu had first responded to the sight of his bride-to-be's photograph. According to the servant, he had frowned and muttered with distaste, "Country bumpkin." That discovery led Youyi to believe that her husband had decided to dislike her from the start. Xu, it turned out, had envisioned a modern love marriage for himself, not an arranged one, no matter how accommodating his bride might be.

Soon after the wedding Xu set off alone to resume his education. From 1915 to 1918 he studied at Shanghai Baptist College and Theological Seminary, Peiyang University in Tianjin, and Peking University. During these years he pursued coursework in political science and law in preparation to go into business, only dabbling in the arts and humanities as a side interest.

LIANG QICHAO

(FEBRUARY 23, 1873–JANUARY 19, 1929)

Liang Qichao was a Chinese scholar, journalist, philosopher, and reformer of China's imperial rule. Born into a family of farmers in Xinhui, Guangdong Province, he was educated primarily by his father and grandfather. Liang was introduced to literary works early on, and by age six he was writing thousand-word-long essays. He passed his first civil service examination when he was only eleven.

Liang was a disciple of the Confucian scholar and reformist Kang Youwei, and he soon became an advocate of constitutional monarchy, which he hoped would change the way the Qing government ruled. He and Kang advocated for industrializing the economy, introducing Western subjects into traditional school curriculums and ending practices such as foot binding and opium smoking. They also proposed a particular vision for a constitutional government and sent their proposal to Emperor Guangxu. With the emperor's support, the proposal inspired a movement called the Hundred Days' Reform. The ensuing debates and uproar over these proposed changes prompted the Empress Dowager Cixi to terminate the reforms, place Emperor Guangxu under house arrest, and send Liang into exile in Japan for thirteen years.

While in Japan, Liang wrote prolifically on Western thought and continued to advance democratic ideas. His popularity soared during this period, and the publications he wrote for were often smuggled into China for circulation. Liang also traveled around the world meeting with such leaders as U.S. President Theodore Roosevelt and Australian Prime Minister Edmund Barton. He returned to China after the overthrow of the Qing dynasty in 1911 to form the Progressive Party and eventually fought against President Yuan Shikai's attempt to become the next Chinese emperor.

As a journalist, Liang communicated his political ideas through newspapers and magazines. When he served as editor in chief of the *New Citizen Journal*, he explained that he viewed newspapers as "mirrors of society" and endeavored to produce a "newspaper of the world" that served "the best interests of all humanity."

Along these lines of thought, Liang challenged China's traditional perspective on history and fostered a social awareness of the need to modernize; he believed this was necessary to forge a strong and just nation. Liang also oversaw the translation of many Western works into Chinese, which he believed was essential to China's progress. He studied Western philosophers of the Enlightenment period, such as John Stuart Mill and Jean-Jacques Rousseau, and translated their works into Chinese.

In 1919 he attended the Paris Peace Conference, where he became greatly disillusioned with the West—not only because of the Western allies' decision to concede Chinese territory to Japan but also because of their preoccupation with science and materialism. In the late 1920s Liang retired from politics and devoted his life to teaching at Nankai University (Tianjin University) as a professor of history. He brought many intellectual figures to China, such as the German philosopher Hans Driesch and the Indian poet Rabindranath Tagore. Through his writings, Liang challenged traditional Chinese thought and built the foundation for the later intellectual revolution of the May Fourth era. He deeply influenced many of his students, including Xu Zhimo. His most notable publications include *Introduction to the Learning of the Qing Dynasty*, *History of Chinese Culture*, *Selected Essays of Yinbingshi*, and *The Construction of New China*. He is widely considered one of the most important intellectual leaders of early twentieth-century China.

Liang had one wife and one concubine, who together bore him nine children. His second son, Liang Sicheng, married Lin Huiyin, the daughter of Lin Changmin, with whom Liang had served in the cabinet of the warlord Duan Qirui. Liang died in Shanghai on January 19, 1929, at age fifty-five.

CHAPTER THREE

EXPLORING
THE WEST

1918–1921

IN SEARCH OF A DESTINY,
A JOURNEY TO AMERICA

n 1918 Youyi and Xu, then twenty-one, welcomed a son. But this family addition was not enough to tether the scholar to domestic life. His intellectual drive remained in full force. He was developing formative relationships that would feed and support his ambitions. Youyi's family introduced Xu to Liang Qichao, who has been credited with bringing Western economic ideas to China. Liang became Xu's mentor and inspired him with dreams of making a lasting impact on his nation. Xu began to envision a future as China's version of Alexander Hamilton, who is often credited with developing America's financial system. With these grand ambitions in mind, Liang encouraged his young prodigy to travel abroad and develop a wider perspective on life and the world. Liang's urging was fully in step with the Chinese zeitgeist. The nation's intellectuals had founded the **New Culture Movement**, a widespread attempt to cultivate a progressive Chinese culture based on global and Western standards.

During the 1870s and 1880s, the Qing government began sending young scholars abroad for educational missions that were part of yet another national

Xu at Clark College, Worcester, Massachusetts, where he studied history and graduated with high honors.

initiative, the Self-Strengthening Movement. Dynastic officials believed that in order to maintain China's position in the modern world, the country's youth would need to embrace Western technical knowledge and Western learning in general. Many of the brightest and most privileged students went abroad to study in America and England, but an increasing number of Chinese scholars were heading to Japan and France. In 1915 there were more than one thousand Chinese studying in America. The first wave of Chinese students to arrive in America were financially sponsored by the **Boxer Indemnity Scholarship Program**, possibly the most successful of the foreign-study movements in China. After the 1910s, however, many Chinese students in the United States were self-funded. That was certainly true in Xu Zhimo's case; his successful father fully supported these early years of education abroad.

Xu expressed concern to his family about the loneliness he might experience in moving abroad by himself and the uncertainty that lay ahead. Yet, a sizable number of upper-class Chinese students were heading to the West, gaining a broader range of ideas became essential for young men of his standing. Thus, even at that early age, Xu Zhimo most likely understood that staying in China without any foreign experience would seriously limit the scope of his thinking and quite possibly his future role in China as well.

In the summer of 1918 Xu left his wife and newborn with his parents and boarded a ship bound for the United States. He had enrolled as a transfer student at Clark College in Worcester, Massachusetts, to earn a bachelor of arts in history. Besides founding one of the first graduate schools in America, Clark also attracted a number of outstanding foreign scholars. Thus, with a combination of humility and high expectations, the young Xu embarked on a voyage that would fundamentally alter his life and point of view.

While aboard the ship, he wrote a letter about China to his parents and friends. Composed in Classical Chinese, it offers insight into Xu's complex mind and his deep desire to take China forward. It reflects his patriotism and idealism and also his sense of hope for his country's future:

> Each year more and more of our countrymen have been going abroad in search of an education. When they return, some go into political life, some go into the world of practical affairs, and some cannot decide what to do. Those in the first category have plenty of ability but are blinded in their search for profit; those in the second category have plenty of knowledge but cannot tell how to apply it; those in the third category either are helpless as fish on dry land or

else are trying to find a right way in hopeless circumstances. Alas! These people are our nation's treasure, and yet their confusion and chaos has reached this extent. How can we have no true patriots? . . . Instead, they wander around irresolute and follow the old ways. . . . They must understand that today's heroes cannot avoid the tempests [of China's brewing political upheavals].

For weeks, the twenty-one-year-old Xu, a solitary figure in a padded silk jacket and round black-framed spectacles, stood at the ship's bow, watching the gray ocean pass beneath him.

Upon his arrival in the United States, Xu began his studies at Clark College. He took courses in economics and history and found a small circle of expatriate Chinese students who chose to follow a demanding schedule of rising at dawn for exercise and study. They met often to discuss their ambitious plans for China's future. Several years before, during his time at Peiyang University, Xu had adopted the Western name Hamilton with the hope that he would follow in the footsteps of Alexander Hamilton. In 1919 he graduated from Clark with high honors. Soon afterward he left that traditional collegiate setting and headed to the sophisticated metropolis of New York, where he would pursue a master's degree in political science at Columbia University.

At Columbia, Xu continued his studies in history and economics; he also pursued coursework in political theory, immersing himself in Owenite socialism and the history of the Russian Revolution. His graduate thesis was titled "The Status of Women in China"—an interesting choice of topics given the drama-filled relationships he would later have with the women in his life. In this academic work he argued that missionary reports about female oppression in China had been exaggerated. Historians examining this period of Xu's life conclude that the young scholar was clearly priming himself for a future as an economist, a devoted disciple of Liang Qichao, and a successor to his banking- and business-magnate father.

However, neither this course of study nor life in America's most developed city fulfilled Xu's sense of self and mission. In an essay he wrote years later, he looked back on this period with ambivalence: "In America I kept busy attending classes, listening to lectures, writing exams, chewing gum, going to the movies, and swearing." He also criticized himself for not developing his intellect more during his New York sojourn. "If I were a pure dunce when I came to America, I remained unchanged when I parted from the Lady of Liberty." He rebelled against the comfort and complacency he believed he had embraced during that period and began to consider an intellectual and emotional alliance with another country, England.

During his Clark and Columbia years, Xu continued to discuss politics and societal upheaval in China ardently. Of particular focus was 1919's **May Fourth Movement**, during which about five thousand university students in Beijing protested against the terms imposed by the Treaty of Versailles that was signed at the Paris Peace Conference on April 28, 1919. The historic post-World War I agreement reached by the Allied Powers' leaders awarded Japan the former German leasehold of Qingdao in China's Shandong Province. Xu's mentor, Liang Qichao, was in Paris during these negotiations and sent telegram updates about the negotiations home to China. Intellectuals, including Liang, saw the treaty as a reflection of China's tarnished international reputation—a country becoming increasingly weak and insular, a failure in the modern era. On May 1, a Beijing newspaper published the news that the final Versailles settlements had gone against China. On May 4, protests erupted in Beijing in the form of riots and demonstrations. The outrage then spread to Shanghai, with the Chinese declaring a national boycott of Japanese goods.

The May Fourth Movement took on a huge significance for all Chinese, including Xu. The movement barreled through China, opening up the country to new and diverse ways of looking at all aspects of society—from education to labor unions, from art to women's rights—as everything cultural and political became open to new interpretations and reforms. Students and intellectuals passionately discussed and embraced ideas from the West. Even writing in the vernacular, as opposed to Classical Chinese, became acceptable. This push for cultural and social progress would play a major role in Xu's own writing and thinking when he eventually returned to China. He became one of its forward-thinking leaders, certainly on the literary front, in a country experiencing new ways of exploring and redefining its societal foundations.

A SHIFT IN ALLEGIANCES

Xu initially considered pursuing a doctoral degree at Columbia. However, he found himself feeling both restless and somewhat disillusioned with the United States. Thus, in 1920, he decided to leave America behind for England. His primary goal in relocating to the U.K. was to study with *Bertrand Russell*, the notable and controversial English philosopher, logician, and social critic. Liang Qichao had introduced Xu to the writings of philosophers such as Friedrich Nietzsche and Russell, and their work captivated the young man.

Russell was from an aristocratic British family—his father was a viscount, his grandfather a prime minister. Xu, also from an upper-class family, seemed to draw deep inspiration from his iconoclastic thinking. Russell wrote that three passions governed his decisions and actions: "the longing for love, the search for knowledge and the unbearable pity for the suffering of mankind." This was a perspective that Xu, in turn, seemed to admire and adopt as his own.

Especially interesting was Russell's conviction that foreign powers should not control the economic destiny of any other country; in particular he spoke out against the tussle between Europe and Japan for control over China, which the philosopher had visited in 1920. Russell's writings clearly had a profound impact on Xu. The young scholar now sensed an unbreakable thread connecting him to England and its writers and philosophers.

While still at Columbia, Xu heard that Russell had died from pneumonia during a yearlong speaking tour of China and Japan. The news of his hero's sudden death shook him deeply. Even though at that time he had never met the lauded philosopher, Xu wept and composed a memorial poem in his honor.

It soon came to light, however, that the rumors were false. Russell had indeed become gravely ill with double pneumonia and phlebitis during his trip to China, but he had eventually recovered. And yet, despite the philosopher's widely publicized lecture in the island country, the Japanese did not report his return to a healthy state, causing international speculation about his death to amplify.

Russell was not pleased with the Japanese news corps' omission of his recovery in the national press, seeing it as inconsiderate and irresponsible. He and his soon-to-be second wife, Dora Black, decided to exact some small revenge on the Japanese in the form of a prank. When Tokyo journalists approached the philosopher for an interview, Black handed them each a typewritten slip that stated that Russell "was dead" and therefore "could not be interviewed." In his three-volume tome *The Autobiography of Bertrand Russell*, published in parts in the 1950s and 1960s, the philosopher wrote that upon receiving the note, the Japanese journalists looked down at the message and then up at Russell, clearly alive, and muttered, "Ah! Vereee funnee!"

Russell was indeed alive, news that inspired Xu to cancel his dissertation course at Columbia and board a ship headed to London. Xu vowed "to apply myself wholeheartedly to studying with this twentieth-century Voltaire." He later wrote an essay titled "The Cambridge I Knew" that explained his decision to leave his settled American life:

> In the ups and downs of my life I have usually been tugged by the strings of deep emotion—we can take my search for education as one example. I went to England because I wanted to be a follower of Russell.

The move across the Atlantic may have seemed relatively effortless to Xu, then a young man with few responsibilities other than to enrich himself academically, but it was a decision that would set a new life course in motion.

ENGLAND AND A NEW DIRECTION

Xu reached England in October 1920 in hopes of working with Russell at Cambridge University, where the philosopher had been a fellow at Trinity College. As it turned out, however, Russell was still on his extended trip to China and Japan. Xu's hopes were further dashed when he learned that Russell's university colleagues had forced him to leave his post at Trinity several years before, in 1916. They could not condone his pacifist views during World War I. His recent divorce added to their negative judgment of him.

Xu chose to settle in London instead, shifting his intellectual intentions to studying political science at the London School of Economics. During this time he wrote a number of essays about politics for Liang Qichao's journal, *New Citizen*. But while he made concerted efforts to engage in China's politics, he discovered that he was not truly invested in the subject. About this period Xu wrote: "It was a time when I was . . . deeply depressed and looking for new directions."

Sensing Xu's isolation and rudderless state from the tone of his letters, Liang introduced his young protégé to another London-based Chinese, **Lin Changmin**, a representative of the Chinese League of Nations Union, a nongovernmental organization. Liang and Lin Changmin had served together in the cabinet of Duan Qirui, a Chinese warlord, in 1917. Although Lin Changmin was twenty years older than Xu, the two formed a close friendship, one based on shared intellectual and emotional passions. Lin went as far as confiding in Xu about an early love affair he had had with a Japanese girl he met while studying in Japan. Historians have theorized that Lin's admission might have awakened

Xu's own romantic yearnings, as well as the realization that he could look beyond his traditionally arranged marriage for love. The two began to write playful love letters to each other, Xu penning his missives from the perspective of a married woman and Lin returning the communiqués in the voice of a married man. Acts such as these reflect Xu's exuberant personality and his willingness to experiment socially.

Xu became a steady presence at the Lin house and, in the process, grew fond of Lin's daughter, **Lin Huiyin**, seven years his junior. The relationship began as a polite one, with the young girl initially referring to the older scholar as Uncle Xu. But as the pair grew to know each other, their connection shifted. Xu admired the girl's quick wit, deep interest in literature, artistic talent, and vivacity, as well as her delicate beauty. In time, Xu fell profoundly in love with Huiyin. With a passionate in-the-flesh creature such as Huiyin in his presence, Xu let his sense of obligation to his wife and young son float away.

But at sixteen, Huiyin was not at an age where she could reciprocate Xu's love. She was a schoolgirl living in her father's house. In addition, Lin Changmin had been considering many illustrious marriage matches for her. This, however, would not dissuade Xu from pursuing and pining for her.

BERTRAND RUSSELL

(MAY 18, 1872–FEBRUARY 2, 1970)

Bertrand Arthur William Russell was a renowned British author, philosopher, logician, and mathematician whose international reputation inspired Xu Zhimo to leave America and journey to England in the hopes of becoming one of his tutees. Russell believed in free trade and anti-imperialism, and he was an antiwar activist who went to prison for his pacifism during World War I. He socialized often with the Bloomsbury Group.

Russell was born into one of the most prominent aristocratic families in Britain. His grandfather served as Prime Minister under Queen Victoria and his family's rise to power can be traced back to the Tudor dynasty. However, Russell suffered tragedy early on in life: his mother and sister died when he was two, followed by the death of his father two years later. In their absence, he and his brother were brought up by his paternal grandparents and educated by governesses and tutors, studying French and German. As a teenager Russell was greatly influenced by the works of John Stuart Mill (his secular godfather) and Percy Bysshe Shelley and ultimately declared himself an atheist. He later attended Trinity College, Cambridge, where he was a brilliant student of mathematics and philosophy. He became a fellow of the college in 1895.

In 1903 Russell wrote *The Principles of Mathematics*, which was later expanded into the three-volume *Principia Mathematica*. This research established Russell as a founding father of modern analytical philosophy. He began lecturing at Cambridge University in 1910. Russell continued to write many essays on moral and psychological topics, which ultimately led to his masterwork, *History of Western Philosophy*. He also wrote *The Practice and Theory of Bolshevism*, *The Problem of China*, and *Proposed Roads to Freedom: Socialism, Anarchism, and Syndicalism*.

Being a descendant of the Whig aristocracy, Russell delighted in standing up for his radical convictions. For example, in 1916 he was deprived of his lectureship at Trinity College after his pacifist activities brought him into conflict with the government. He went to prison for six months, where he wrote his *Introduction to Mathematical Philosophy*. Russell traveled to China in the fall of 1920 and spent a year at Peking University lecturing on philosophy.

When he and Xu met in 1921, Russell was in the midst of obtaining a divorce from his first wife, Alys Pearsall Smith, as he had fallen in love with the feminist writer Dora Black. He would eventually marry four times: to Smith in 1894, to Black in 1921, to Patricia Helen Spence in 1935, and finally to Edith Finch in 1952. The impact of Russell's unabashed pursuit of romantic love on Xu cannot be underestimated. Knowing the great lengths to which Russell went to secure his divorce from Smith (which was still a controversial matter in Britain at that time), Xu was likely inspired to forge a similar course when he requested a divorce from Youyi.

Though his views were controversial and often criticized by peers, Russell remained dedicated to social and political activism. He was awarded the Nobel Prize in Literature in 1950. He died of influenza in Wales in 1970 at the age of ninety-seven.

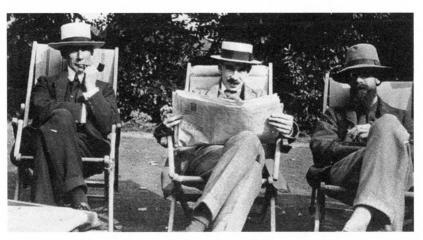

Russell at a gathering with John Maynard Keynes and Lytton Strachey.

CHAPTER FOUR

THE CAMBRIDGE YEARS

1921–1922

DICKINSON AND A STORIED UNIVERSITY

During these early days in London, Lin Changmin introduced Xu to *Goldsworthy Lowes Dickinson*, a notable writer, intellectual, and fellow at King's College, Cambridge. Dickinson often described himself as a socialist with a staunch dislike of the established social order. He wrote the well-received 1902 book *Letters from John Chinaman*, a work of fiction written in the voice of an educated Chinese man. In the book the narrator defends his country's widespread refusal to allow Western influences to permeate Chinese society. It is interesting to note that Dickinson had not visited China before he wrote the book, and yet he demonstrated a deep understanding of the culture.

In 1911 Dickinson finally traveled to China. During this time, he visited the sacred Mount Tai as well as the area where Confucius lived. He climbed the mountain, camping along the trail so that he could witness the sunsets and sunrises. The experience gave him deep insight into the Chinese ethos. Of his trek up the sacred mountain and his experience of the country, he wrote in his book of essays *Appearances*, "A people that can so consecrate a place of natural beauty is a people of fine feeling for the essential values of life."

Xu's Cambridge years were among the happiest of his life. As a student on campus, Xu began formally writing poetry in 1921.

This journey to China inspired Dickinson to compose a series of poems about his experience in the Middle Kingdom. This shared passion for the country fostered a deep connection between him and Xu. Despite their thirty-five-year age difference, the two developed a remarkable friendship. The pair spent many afternoons in animated discussion, Dickinson in his three-piece wool suit and Xu in his flowing silk Manchu robe. Dickinson offered Xu entry to an elite circle: the upper-class intellectuals of London. In turn, Xu, whose English was flawless and his thinking complex even at age twenty-four, offered Dickinson an uncommon glimpse into the Chinese mind. As a gesture of friendship, Xu gave Dickinson, who he called Goldie, a silk Chinese cap, and the Englishman wore it regularly. Dickinson quickly became one of Xu's most trusted advisers.

Dickinson suggested to his young friend that he leave his course of study at the London School of Economics and pursue a graduate degree at the fabled King's College. Since it was too late to enroll for that year, Xu joined King's College as an independent study student instead. Unable to secure on-campus housing in the college's limestone halls, Xu rented a small cottage in the nearby village of Sawston and traveled the six miles to campus daily by bicycle.

He still frequently took the train into London to visit Lin Changmin and Huiyin, whom Xu continued to pursue ardently. Huiyin returned the affection in letters, but her studies at St. Mary's College, a London preparatory school, as well as her father's disapproval, kept her from fully engaging in the romance.

HUSBAND AND WIFE REUNITE, BUT NOT HAPPILY

Xu's daily existence had at this point been one of quiet reflection and intellectual stimulation, filled with the ease and graces of polite society. But life was about to become exponentially more difficult. Youyi's brother had convinced Xu's parents that the couple should be reunited, lest they grow apart.

During his absence from China, Xu had maintained his ties to his parents. He wrote home frequently, always addressing the letters to them, rather than his wife, which was customary. In one letter he asked Youyi to follow their son, Jikai, for an entire day and report on the toddler's actions. She happily complied, taking note of everything he did or said. She later told her biographer she had been grateful for the opportunity to make a connection with her husband.

After some consideration, the family decided that Youyi would join her husband in England, but Jikai would remain with the family in their Xiashi compound. Youyi took a five-week journey on a steamship to France, her first trip abroad. Throughout the long voyage she felt a mounting excitement about seeing Xu.

It was a sentiment that would not be returned. Decades later she would recall to her biographer that when she landed in Marseille and met her husband at the docks, she saw in his eyes not love, but disdain. She said that she felt she was little more than an unwelcome visitor from China. Of course, the couple did share moments of lightness and intimacy. For example, when they flew from Marseille to London—Youyi's first plane ride ever—she became so airsick she vomited, prompting Xu to call her a "country bumpkin." A few moments later, Xu himself threw up, which led Youyi to mutter back, "Who's the country bumpkin?"

Almost immediately, it became clear to both Xu and Youyi that three years of life alone in the West had changed him. In America and England he had experienced freedom of movement and thought. Through his exchanges with notable

Xu and Youyi, four months after
Youyi's arrival in England.

philosophers and intellectuals, he had begun to feel staunchly that arranged marriages, rather than those founded on passion, were archaic; such unions were relics of unenlightened societies and not in any way modern. What's more, the presence of a wife made it difficult for Xu to carry on with the social life he had established in England. He now faced the prospect of living a double life.

Once the couple settled into Xu's Sawston cottage, Youyi noticed that the scholar began acting oddly. On the mornings when he did not depart for campus, he rushed out to the barbershop, sometimes claiming to get a haircut every few days. In reality, he was heading to the local grocery store, where he checked for letters from Huiyin and wrote his own impassioned missives in return.

It is interesting to note that Huiyin was the result of her father's relationship with a concubine, which reflects the prevailing Chinese traditions of the era. When Lin Changmin's wife from an arranged marriage was not able to bear him any children, he took a concubine, who bore him a son and two daughters. The son died in infancy, and one daughter died in early childhood, leaving Huiyin as the sole survivor of this arrangement. Her father would later take yet another concubine who would bear him another daughter and four sons. Throughout all of this Huiyin would remain her father's favorite, accompanying him on his many travels, including to London, where she met Xu.

Sometime in 1921 Xu reportedly suggested marriage to Huiyin. She firmly told him she would not give him an answer until he had divorced his wife. Soon afterward, Xu discovered that Lin Changmin had taken his daughter back to China without saying goodbye—a discovery that left Xu reeling emotionally.

BERTRAND RUSSELL'S PROFOUND INFLUENCE

Xu met Bertrand Russell in London in 1921, and their intellectual exchange influenced him significantly. In the midst of the emotional upheaval caused by Huiyin's sudden departure, he deepened his correspondence with Russell. The philosopher had tried desperately to divorce his first wife, Alys Pearsall Smith, in order to marry Dora Black, a feminist author and social campaigner he had met on a weekend walking tour.

Divorce was still very much a controversial issue at the time, even in the West. Although Smith readily agreed to Russell's request to part ways, the process was hardly as simple as filing papers in the court. The parties involved had to prove that a "wrong" had been committed. Thus, Russell arranged to meet a female friend, the English writer and actor Colette O'Niel, at a London hotel, and the two staged what appeared to be an adulterous affair for Smith's lawyers. A few weeks later he invited detectives hired by Smith's solicitors to observe him checking into yet another hotel, this time with Black—proof of a public night of infidelity.

Only then did judges agree to the divorce. The split led to much peer criticism of Russell. By the time Xu met him, he and Black were married and expecting a child. No doubt Russell's pursuit of romantic love over obligation influenced Xu deeply.

While considering the choice of following one's passion over tradition, Xu also took inspiration from the romantic poet Shelley, who had abandoned his wife and eloped with seventeen-year-old Mary Godwin (the daughter of the philosopher William Godwin and the future author of *Frankenstein; or, The Modern Prometheus*). From his study of the romantic poets, Xu began to draw strength and motivation from the idea of a poet's soul being different from the average man's. He also gave credence to the idea that artists have a profound need for emotional freedom and passion, a path that would demand defying social boundaries.

Xu was at a crossroads. On one hand, he had been groomed to be the dutiful son, adhering to Confucian traditions of filial piety, marital responsibilities, and duty to his country. On the other, he understood that a break from traditional ties could lead him to something greater: creative fulfillment and an honest emotional life.

At that time, Chinese society viewed marriage as an alliance between families, rather than as a uniting of passionate souls. Romantic love existed, of course, but it was not what marriages were based upon. As for divorce, there were examples of people leaving a spouse, but it was a rare occurrence and considered extremely improper. The Chinese had established grounds for legal separation—for example, men could divorce their wives if they failed to bear a son, or if they objected to their husbands taking additional wives or concubines—but it was far more common to remain married, if only in name. An actual legal divorce was very rare. Thus, for Xu to even consider divorce—for the sake of romantic love, no less—would have seemed bizarre, even shocking, at the time. Chinese society would have viewed the choice not as a personal act but as one with great social and political symbolism.

While he was contemplating this radical social decision, fate threw Xu another curve. Youyi became pregnant with their second child. Despite his emotional defection to Huiyin, Xu had continued to have marital relations with his wife. His heart remained steadfast, however. He asked Youyi to have an abortion, a radical and dangerous procedure at the time and one she refused. He tried desperately to convince his wife of their incompatibility. At one point the normally even-tempered Xu even shouted at her, "Bound feet and Western dress do not go together." And that was despite the fact that Youyi was actually the first woman in her family to escape having her feet bound. Feeling increasingly trapped, Xu left the Sawston cottage one morning and never returned, leaving his pregnant twenty-one-year-old wife alone.

Xu moved onto the university campus, six miles away from Sawston, where he finally was able to immerse himself in Cambridge life. He spent his days doing what most privileged students in the West did: strolling through the countryside, punting down the River Cam, bicycling, smoking, chatting with friends over tea and buttered pastries, and indulging his love of reading. "Only then did I have the opportunity to be in close touch with the real Cambridge, and simultaneously discover Cambridge—a greater pleasure than I have ever known," he wrote.

It was during this time that scholars believe Xu, then twenty-four, wrote his first formal poem. Dated November 1921, "The Dewdrops on the Grass" reflects, among other things, that Xu had begun to see himself as a poet, with high aspirations as a literary artist.

> O poet!
>> Prophet of the spirit age,
>> Consummator of ideas and the arts,
>> Creator between heaven and man,
>
>> The materials you work with include rivers, seas, wind, clouds,
>> Birds, animals, flowers, grass, gods, demons, flies, mosquitoes;
>> In short, all things celestial, terrestrial and human;

Years later Xu would look back on this period in his life and consider the life-changing transformation that had taken place at Cambridge. The loss of Huiyin, combined with his immersion in nature and his blossoming as a poet, had caused him to change in profound ways.

Of his early poems, he wrote:

> There was only one period in which my poetic sentiments were
> somewhat like a flood unleashed suddenly from the mountains,
> dashing violently without any direction. That was the first six

months of my career as a poet when my life was so shaken by a tremendous force that my ideas, half-mature and immature, were promptly rendered into muddled lines of poetry. Without any model to follow or a care in the world, I indiscriminately gave vent to whatever pent-up feelings were accumulated in my heart. I wrote with such a great urgency as if I were trying to save someone from destruction, paying no heed to quality! In a short time, a great deal of such poetry was produced, but almost all of it was unworthy of publication.

Of this time he also wrote: "I came across a strange wind, or was shone on by some strange moonlight, and since then my thought has turned to the expression of words in lines. A profound melancholy finally overpowered me. This melancholy, I believe, even gradually permeated and transformed my temperament."

Xu could feel himself changing as he began to understand the strange artistic power growing within him. Allowing other half-formed identities of banker, economist, and family successor to fall off his shoulders, he had now settled on a new identity and a fate: that of a poet.

Xu had abandoned his wife and unborn child, and yet he had not completely abandoned his filial ties or old value system. That much became evident when he sent his friend Wang Zimei to the Sawston cottage to speak to Youyi. Xu's envoy asked Youyi, who was at the end of her first trimester of pregnancy, if she would consider being a "daughter-in-law to the Xu family, but not Xu Zhimo's wife." Wang then explained to Youyi that Xu had sent him to deliver a devastating message: "He does not want you."

One cannot ignore the coldness of Xu toward his wife. Looking back on her husband's actions, Youyi said, "If Xu Zhimo's words were any indication of his thoughts or spirit, he was not the man I had married, the one who wrote dutiful letters home to his parents and obeyed their wishes to treat me like a wife. He was a different man altogether, one Western not just in clothing but in outlook as well. I was bewildered by this change in him. How did it happen?" Four months pregnant, Youyi left England to live with her brother in Berlin. She later told her biographer that at that point, she decided that she, too, would make modern decisions for her own life and those of her children. From that time onward, she resolved to rely only on herself. In February 1922 she gave birth to a second son. Although Youyi gave her son the Chinese name Desheng, she called him by his English name, Peter.

GOLDSWORTHY LOWES DICKINSON

(AUGUST 6, 1862–AUGUST 3, 1932)

Goldsworthy Lowes Dickinson was a British historian, political philosopher, and peace activist who became Xu Zhimo's mentor and good friend. Dickinson was born in London to a portrait painter father and a literary agent mother. Educated at King's College, Cambridge, Class of 1884, he was an outstanding scholar who won the Chancellor's Medal for a poem he wrote.

He was inducted into the Cambridge Conversazione Society, a club that once included Alfred Lord Tennyson and Arthur Hallam and served as the model for the Bloomsbury Group, of which he also became a member. It was there that he met painter Roger Fry, with whom he fell in love; the relationship was never consummated but the two remained lifelong friends.

At Cambridge, where he would spend the majority of his life, Dickinson immersed himself in works on classical and modern civilization, reading Plato, Shelley, and Goethe. He studied medicine, though he never practiced, wrote poetry that he dismissed as not very good, and pursued humanitarian projects, such as working on a cooperative farm. In 1887 he was named a fellow at Cambridge and lectured there in political science until he retired in 1920. He also taught at the London School of Economics for fifteen years during his tenure at Cambridge.

In 1900 he traveled to Greece, and then went on lecture tours in the United States, India, China, and Japan. It was during these trips that he became aware of the problems caused by Western imperialism and colonialism. He then developed a new concept of civilization shaped by humanism, Oriental philosophy, mystical religion, and classical wisdom. Before he had ever stepped foot in China, Dickinson published *Letters from John Chinaman* in 1901, a fictional account written from the point of view of a Chinese man in defense of traditional Confucian mores and China's refusal to sanction the influx of Western influences.

In fact, he spent much of his life trying to bridge cultural and political divides and promote peace and understanding. At the beginning of World War I he formed the pacifist Bryce Group and joined Bertrand Russell in his antiwar stance. He then advocated for the League of Nations, a name he coined, and was instrumental in its conception. His hope was that the organization would help end warfare around the world.

Xu and Dickinson were introduced by Lin Changmin in 1921, and despite the thirty-five-year age difference, the two became close friends. Dickinson could often be seen walking the grounds of Cambridge wearing a silk Chinese cap, a gift from Xu.

Dickinson wrote many books, including *The Greek Way of Life*; *Plato and His Dialogues*; *War: Its Nature, Cause and Cure*; *A Modern Symposium*; and *After the War*. He never married, and he died after a prostate operation in London on August 3, 1932. Dickinson's good friend E. M. Forster was appointed as his literary executor and, at the beseeching of Dickinson's sisters, wrote and published his biography in 1934.

Dickinson in 1922, around the time he and Xu first struck up a friendship.

CHAPTER FIVE

A NEW MAN
EMERGES

1922

A MODERN DIVORCE

Shortly after Peter's birth, Xu sent Youyi a letter formally asking her for a divorce. As if writing a manifesto against arranged marriages, he told her that their passionless marriage should not be permitted to continue, and that "to redeem freedom with freedom" would enable them both to see again "life's light of dawn." Marriage not based on romantic love was, he declared, "intolerable." He further explained:

> Changing night into day and hell into paradise can be promptly achieved. . . . True life must be attained through struggle; true love, too, must be attained through struggle! Your future and mine are unbounded. . . . You and I have our minds set on reforming society and creating welfare for mankind. Hence we must first set ourselves as examples by freely terminating our marital relationship with courageous resoluteness and intelligent decisiveness, and with mutual respect for each other's personal character. Herein lie both the end of our suffering and the beginning of our happiness.

Xu finds a new direction as a poet
and a single man.

Youyi did not share those convictions, instead preferring to keep their family intact. However, Xu felt his ideals and support of modern choices were more important. A month later, Xu visited Youyi in Berlin in hopes of convincing her to sign divorce papers. As Youyi later said, she believed that her husband's ultimate aim was based less on high ideals than on lovesickness. From her perspective, he wanted to undo his marital ties so that he could pursue Huiyin as a free man.

For the purpose of convincing his wife to terminate their marriage, Xu asked Youyi to come to a friend's house in the city. When she arrived she found Xu and a few Chinese friends standing around. They seemed excited, as if they were waiting to witness a momentous event. Youyi capitulated and signed the divorce papers, and afterward Xu said, "Wonderful, wonderful. You see, this is so necessary. China must rid itself of the old ways." Xu's friends gathered around and shook his hand. Clearly, everyone in the room knew the significance of that moment. Xu had just obtained the first modern divorce in Chinese history.

The poet understood he could not be fully modern if he was married to an arranged partner. While he certainly felt a familial connection to Youyi, he knew that their relationship would not inspire the passionate love he imagined and to which he aspired.

As Xu's fame grew in the years to come, his groundbreaking divorce would become a symbol of societal progress and freedom. His audacious breaking of marital ties may have accelerated the transition of Chinese marriage from a traditional framework into a more modern, Western-style relationship—one that included individual happiness, freedom, and divorce as an alternative way of ending an unwanted connection to another person.

During that Berlin trip, Xu visited his newborn son in the hospital's nursery. It would be the first and only time he would see Peter.

CAMBRIDGE, ONCE MORE

While the divorce was certainly a monumental event for Xu, it was the young scholar's life at Cambridge and his growing passion for writing that now defined him. He had returned to the university town in the spring of 1922, a season he later characterized as his most memorable phase of life: "Only during that spring my life was natural and truly happy, although it chanced to be also the period during which I experienced most of life's agony." He often took a tram to classes, studied in the stately King's College library, and ate at inexpensive cafés. In this way, he assumed the life of a young Western scholar, not a married Chinese man with children. "It was during this time that I gradually 'discovered' Cambridge," he wrote. "Never had I known a greater joy."

Liberated from his marriage and his debilitating domestic situation at the Sawston cottage, Xu was free to enjoy the beauty and excitement of Cambridge. He loved reading and writing under the willows and oaks that lined the River Cam. He spent hours at a time gazing at the water, lying on the grass and watching the drifting clouds—what he called "nature's brocade."

> Only rarely is the rising sun visible on these days of early spring. But when it does break through, the early riser knows no greater delight. In an instant the color of the fields deepens, a gold powder like a film of gauze dusts the grass, the trees, the roads, the farms. In an instant the land all about is tenderly suffused with the opulence of morning. In an instant your own heart drinks in its portion of the glory of the dayspring, "Spring!" the victorious air seems to whisper by your ear. "Spring!" your joyful soul seems to echo back.

> Pick any direction you like, take any road you like, go along with the gentle grass-flavored breeze, let your wheels bear you far away…

> If birds are your delight, here at hand are songsters of subtlest variety. If children are your delight, guileless youngsters are everywhere in this countryside. If friendship is your delight, here at hand are country folk who cast no suspicious eye on the stranger from afar.

Xu reveled in his newfound solitude. During these months, he was neither tethered to a marriage nor distracted by a love interest, and he found that this companionless life suited him. "Solitude," he wrote, "is a phenomenon to be relished. I sometimes think it is the first condition of any discovery. If you want to discover the real nature of your friend, you must find an opportunity to be alone with him. If you want to discover your own real nature, you must give yourself an opportunity for solitude."

The young Xu, bespectacled and dressed in a Western suit, spent most days peddling his secondhand bicycle past the cows, sheep, and verdant meadows, exuberant, alone, free.

A decade later he wrote about his years there: "My own eyes were opened by Cambridge; my desire to learn was stimulated by Cambridge; the consciousness of my own being was nourished by Cambridge."

Xu also spent these days cultivating friendships with the English literati, many of whom were also associated with the university, and much of his social life revolved around intellectual exchanges with them. Dickinson introduced Xu to H. G. Wells, E. M. Forster, and Thomas Hardy. Xu dined and drank with such authors at various literary clubs. With the artist and art critic Roger Fry, Xu discussed classical Chinese silk paintings and Song dynasty ceramics. With Arthur Waley, the leading translator of Chinese literature, he talked about Tang dynasty poetry.

Bertrand Russell and Xu had become close friends, and the Cambridge student often traveled to London to attend Russell's lectures. In years to come, the elder intellectual sent Xu a copy of his book *The Problem of China* and asked him to discuss its message with his fellow countrymen. In his correspondence to other members of the cultural elite, Russell described Xu as a "highly cultivated Chinese undergraduate, a poet in both English and Chinese."

Indeed, Xu became a fixture of the London and Cambridge intellectual scenes. The charming, quick-witted young man, who alternated between dressing in flowing Chinese robes and natty Western suits, was not only a novel presence but also a bon vivant. It should be noted that few of the Chinese students studying at Cambridge during the same era enjoyed such social success. Xu's rise could be attributed to the fact that he was not only physically striking, clever, and vivacious, but he was also financially well supported. Furthermore, the British literati clearly felt comfortable with the erudite young man, as Xu moved fluidly between Eastern and Western social circles.

In July 1922 Xu enjoyed a short private meeting in Hampstead with Katherine Mansfield, who was dying of tuberculosis. He would later call the visit his "twenty-minute eternal interview." During their time together they discussed Arthur Waley's and Amy Lowell's translations of Chinese poetry. They also discussed Xu's favorite English writers and his plan for when he returned to China. She cautioned him to avoid his country's politics. The meeting not only inspired Xu's own writing; it also led him to translate eight of her short stories for a Chinese audience. When Mansfield passed away about six months after their visit, Xu said he felt a profound sense of loss and penned the poem, "To Mansfield: A Lament," a few stanzas of which are included here:

In the outskirts of ancient Rome there is a cemetery
>Wherein lie the remains of poets dead a century ago;
A century later the wheels of Hades' black carriage
>Again rumble by the green forest of Fontainebleau.

If we say that the universe is a machine devoid of feeling,
>Then why is the ideal, bright like a lamp, flashing ahead?
If we say that the Creator is the manifestation of truth,
>goodness and beauty,
Then why does the rainbow not always stay at the horizon?

Although you and I have met but once—
>The twenty minutes we spent together will never die—
Who can believe that your angelic grace and bearing divine
>Are really gone, like morning dew, forever from us?

BLOOMSBURY, LINKING EAST AND WEST

Xu often fraternized with other members of the Bloomsbury Group, an informal title for a group of friends who were prominent in a number of fields, including art, literature, economics, art criticism, and political and social theory. The Bloomsbury Group included such iconic thinkers and artists as Virginia and Leonard Woolf, Lytton Strachey, Vanessa Bell, Fry, John Maynard Keynes, Clive Bell, Desmond MacCarthy and Forster. The group was woven together through social friendships, but also by way of sexual and familial relationships. The Bloomsburies, as they called themselves, were remarkable for their progressive social views and reformist ideals as well as for a shared passion for living productive lives and overturning social conventions.

Biographer J. K. Johnstone describes the circle as having a "common respect for the things of the spirit; a belief that the inner life of the soul is much more important than the outer life of action or . . . material things; an admiration for the individual and for the virtues of courage, tolerance, and honesty; a desire that man shall be whole and express himself emotionally as well as intellectually; a love of truth and beauty."

Most likely through an introduction from Arthur Waley, Xu met the biographer Lytton Strachey and the art critic Clive Bell. Xu took particular interest in Fry, who orchestrated an English exhibition of paintings by the then-radical Paul Cézanne, Vincent van Gogh, and Paul Gauguin. Fry's influence on Xu is clear; when the poet returned to China, he tried to drum up interest in the works of Cézanne, Henri Matisse, and Pablo Picasso in Shanghai and Beijing.

That Xu was welcomed into such rarefied circles is, ultimately, not that surprising. Here was a Chinese scholar studying at one of the finest Western universities at a time when Europe and America were questing for knowledge about China. He offered an unpredictable perspective to most conversations, pontificating fluidly in English about British and French literature and Chinese politics, history, and culture. Forster would later comment that his meeting with Xu was "one of the most exciting things that had happened" to him.

These intellectuals' feelings about Xu were clearly mutual. In the years to come, Xu would take the inspiration and excitement of the Bloomsbury Group back to China, where, along with other scholars, he would found his own society of intellectuals and artists known as the **Crescent Moon Society**. Like their Western counterparts, the Crescent Moon members challenged the status quo through their art, writing, lectures, and, at times, scandalous personal relationships. Xu's choices in China were watched and commented upon by his intellectual and social peers. As a progressive thinker, Xu made decisions that sometimes surprised and other times shocked his friends and readers. His actions reflected a country poised on the brink of astounding social and political change.

And yet, as buoyed as he was by his life in Cambridge and London, Xu remained tormented by the loss of Huiyin. In "Night," a meditative poem written in 1922, he ruminates over the dichotomy of light and darkness, happiness and pain. In it he wrote, "If you want true reality, seek it by understanding relative emptiness." Light and darkness, idealism and reality—these dueling motifs would become major themes for Xu, both in his writing and in his life.

Several months after his divorce in 1922, Xu found himself longing to return to China and reunite with Huiyin. Once back on his native shores, he would discover not only that his life was in flux but also that his homeland had entered a period of radical transformation.

Change in Chinese urban society had noticeably accelerated after World War I, with the May Fourth Movement marking a turning point. In many ways this was a reaction to the repression and conservatism of the late nineteenth century. For so many young urban Chinese, the country's old structure, with its Confucian values and archaic traditions, appeared to be making China weak.

Xu himself had undergone a radical change during his years abroad. The twenty-one-year-old man who had left China with the intention of learning about the world, and business in particular, was returning to his homeland as a burgeoning poet and man of letters. His identity as a Chinese national and patriot had also shifted. Life in the West had shown him the value of individualism. He now straddled two continents, two cultures, and two perspectives, and his East-West understanding would come to define him as he took his place in early twentieth-century China.

CHAPTER SIX

RETURN TO CHINA

1922–1924

A POET AND THE CONSPIRACIES OF FATE

several months after his Berlin divorce and four years after he first left China for his Clark College education, Xu reached Shanghai by ship on October 15, 1922. Upon landing he made a trip to Xiashi to see his parents. According to interviews with Youyi, Xu's parents said that it had been a difficult reunion. The Xu family was excited to see their son after so many years apart, but they were also, according to Youyi's memoir, "shocked, angered, embarrassed and wounded" by their son's decision to divorce.

After that challenging visit home, Xu swiftly headed to Beijing to see Huiyin. Another intention of his trip was to become involved in the literary and intellectual spheres of the city; during this era, Beijing was the art and liter-

Taken at the Forbidden City, Beijing, this photograph captures the Indian poet Rabindranath Tagore (seated) and his China entourage, including (clockwise from left of Tagore) Lin Huiyin, Kalidas Nag, Xu Zhimo, Leonard Elmhirst, Kshitimohan Sen, Gretchen Green (Elmhirst's friend), Nandalal Bose, and Isabel Ingram (the private tutor of Emperor Puyi's wife).

ary center of China. There he discovered that his former mentor Liang Qichao had already begun encouraging a relationship and suggesting a marital contract between his son Liang Sicheng and Huiyin. It is interesting to note that both Liang Qichao and Lin Changmin (Huiyin's father) were widely viewed as reformers and progressives. Yet when it came to the fate of their children, they bowed to the centuries-old tradition of an arranged marriage.

Liang was greatly displeased that Xu continued his efforts to court Huiyin, the young woman he had chosen for his son. The match had been made informally and enthusiastically between the two prestigious families, and both clans watched carefully over the unfolding of the engagement and marriage plans. Both sides saw Xu's wholehearted pursuit as disruptive.

On January 2, 1923, Liang wrote a long letter to Xu, making clear his admiration for Xu's talents and intellect and his love for his disciple, whom he considered to be almost a son. But he also urged him to reconsider his continued interest in Huiyin and move on to a serious and meaningful life:

> You should know that it is difficult to establish but easy to dissipate oneself. Your age is now the most precious period in life, but also the most dangerous. If you indulge yourself in unattainable dreams, you will, after a few setbacks, lose your interest in life and die in dejection and anonymity. But death is all right compared to the most frightening prospect of neither life nor death, of helpless decadence.

In the same letter Liang reprimanded Xu for his treatment of Youyi since their parting in Berlin. Xu had remained in contact with his former wife, which to Liang showed that he wanted both to separate from her and yet to retain some familial ties. Liang wrote:

> Hitherto, because I thought there had truly been basic incompatibilities between you and your wife (even if you don't want to call her that, I shall continue to do so), I hadn't wanted to pursue the matter [of your divorce] further. But now I gather that since your return to China you have gone on writing to Youyi and continue to sing her praises. Why then did you act as you did? It's really incomprehensible.

In unusually strong language, Xu wrote back justifying his determination to live life in a way that was true to his own beliefs, with the ideals of love, freedom, and beauty as his guide. Clearly, he felt disapproval from all sides:

> That which I have been struggling for with all my might and by braving willingly society's condemnation is not the avoidance of tragic sufferings, but the composure of my conscience, the firm establishment of my personal character, and the salvation of my soul.
>
> Who among men does not seek commonplace virtue? Who is not content with the status quo? Who is not afraid of difficulty and danger? Yet there are people who manage to free themselves by bursting through their encirclement. Does one mean to say that such people do so because they can help it?
>
> I shall search for the only companion of my soul in the vast sea of humanity. If I succeed in my attempt, it will be due to my good fortune; if I fail, it will be due to my fate. That is all there is to it!

Despite this impassioned discussion, when Xu arrived in Beijing he nonetheless pursued Huiyin. She responded coolly to him, choosing instead to spend her days with her intended, Liang Sicheng. It seems likely that she, a prized, well-educated beauty from a prominent family, realized that an illustrious future depended on a circumspect decision. She surely knew that being the daughter-in-law of a famous man was better than being the second wife of a divorced man whose future was not at all certain.

Around this time Xu wrote a poem called "Sad Thoughts" (the first and last stanzas are below) in which, it seems, he attempts to dissuade himself from falling into despair by finding solace from the beauty of the natural world.

> Sad thoughts are in the front courtyard—
>   No, but look!
>   The new vines are dancing coquettishly,
>   The wisteria is bursting with colors
>   The bees are without restraint and the butterflies refuse to
> leave—
> Sad thoughts are not in the front courtyard.

Could it be that sad thoughts are in me—
    In my heart?
    My heart is like an old ghost town
    Where not a single weed will grow.
    It is like a cold spring
    Whose living source is frozen;
    It is like an insect
    In a long and silent hibernation.
No, sad thoughts are not in my heart.

—May 13, 1923

In this poem Xu mined the themes of reality and idealism, as he had throughout his life as a writer.

Even in the midst of personal turmoil, Xu continued to flourish as a poet and essayist, placing poems and essays in such respected publications as the *Morning Post Literary Supplement (Chenbao)* and the *China Times*. He published his poem "Cambridge, Farewell," in the literary supplement of the *China Times* in March 1923. But he encountered a setback when the newspaper's typesetters, confused by the poem's innovative form, ignored the many enjambed lines and added periods instead—an act that infuriated Xu.

Xu relied on established friends to help him professionally. Liang Qichao, for one, continued to advance Xu's career, regardless of his disapproval of Xu's personal life. In fact, Liang, who was in charge of many noteworthy literary projects, became the young intellectual's biggest supporter, recommending him to significant posts, such as editor of the *China Times*'s literary supplement (a position that, in the end, did not materialize).

When Liang became the head of the Songbo Library in Beijing, he appointed Xu to oversee all correspondence in English and gave him a large budget to buy noteworthy Western publications for the library. When the elder scholar and other intellectuals such as **Hu Shi** and Lin Changmin decided to invite the Indian Nobel Laureate ***Rabindranath Tagore*** to visit China, Liang made arrangements for Xu to be Tagore's official interpreter as he toured the country for the first time.

Tagore, Huiyin and Xu during the Indian
poet's first tour of China.

FAME, FRIENDSHIP, AND RABINDRANATH TAGORE

For many of China's scholars, Tagore was not only the face of modern Indian literature but also represented a philosophical bridge between the subcontinent and China. Indeed, the revered Indian poet often stated that one of his life's missions was to build a deeper connection between the great Asian nations.

At this moment, when China was looking outward for new political, social, scientific, and cultural ideas, the country's intellectual cognoscenti turned toward its colonial neighbor India for inspiration. It was to this end that the Beijing Lecture Association, a collective of academics led by Liang, invited Tagore to tour the country and speak about his unifying perspectives. When the Indian philosopher agreed to come, China's intellectual elite set about preparing for a dazzling six-week multi-city tour for him.

The country's literati waited in high anticipation for Tagore's arrival. Many admired the Indian poet for his passionate support of the great civilizations of the East. The hope was that Tagore would bring engaging social ideas and a faceted perspective to a country in search of its international identity.

According to the 2011 book *Tagore and China*, the Indian philosopher was especially invested in developing an Indian-Chinese understanding and brotherhood. He envisioned the two countries rising to take their place in the world, espousing a common vision of leadership. Furthermore, he believed the neighboring nations shared an ingrained cultural focus on the harmonious development of the spirit. In India, this idea was called *vasudhaiva kuntumbakam*, meaning "the world is one family." In China, this philosophy manifested in the concept of *shijie datong*, meaning "the world in grand harmony."

Against this backdrop, Tagore arrived by ship in Shanghai on April 12, 1924. He traveled with a small entourage that included the English philanthropist and agricultural economist **Leonard Elmhirst**, who had appointed himself Tagore's British secretary, and three Bengalis, including the Sanskrit scholar Kshitimohan Sen, lauded artist Nandalal Bose, and the author and parlimentarian Kalidas Nag. Along with hundreds of admiring Chinese students, Xu met the Nobel Laureate and his entourage at the Shanghai docks.

Xu worked both as Tagore's tour liaison and his interpreter, fluidly translating the conversations between English and Chinese. Tagore quickly grew fond of his Chinese aide, reveling in his easy sense of humor and poetic sensibility. Perhaps most importantly, the Indian elder recognized in Xu "a man through whom he felt he could get in touch with the spirit of the Chinese." A palpable empathy flowed between the two poets. Xu later wrote that he had found in Tagore a "great harmonious and beautiful personality, through which one can find inspiration for the culture of India, both ancient and modern."

Before long, Tagore and Xu were writing poetry together. Later in the visit, the pair spent one especially memorable day in Hangzhou, amid the city's landscape of pagodas, lotus flowers, and gardens. Boarding a boat on the West Lake that evening, they discussed and composed poetry until the early hours of the morning.

Moving north to Beijing, Tagore gave six lectures and, with Xu in tow, attended lively private fêtes held in his honor. At the welcoming banquet Liang gave a luminous tribute to India and its rich and complex culture. In Beijing Tagore met another Chinese aide who would accompany him on the tour: it was Huiyin. Fluent in English, she provided him with another perspective on the culture, as well as physical support—she held the sixty-three-year-old poet's arm as she walked to steady him. Tagore, with his flowing white hair and dark wizened face, offered a stunning contrast to his young Chinese companions, Lin Huiyin and Xu. One writer put the sight of the three thusly: "Miss Lin, lovely as a flower, was walking arm in arm with the aged Indian poet, and then there was the long-gowned, pale-faced and slender Xu Zhimo; [the three] resembled a painting of the three friends of winter"—the pine, the bamboo, and the plum blossom.

Tagore turned sixty-three during his China tour. To commemorate this event his traveling companions decided to stage *Chitra*, a one-act play the Indian poet had penned in 1914. In it, Prince Arjuna falls in love with Princess Chitra and asks her father, the king, for her hand in marriage. Huiyin played Chitra, Xu's friend Zhang Xinhai played Arjuna, and Xu stood in for the God of Love. The performance took place in a small hall in Beijing, with Huiyin dressed in full Indian costume. The creative collective that labored to pull off the event eventually formed the Crescent Moon Society; thus, that performance is considered its unofficial founding date.

Tagore was overcome with emotion after witnessing the radiant Huiyin perform his play and went up to the stage to hug her. The poet had heard that his two Chinese companions, Xu and Huiyin, had been in love but had been discouraged from marrying. Soon after, Tagore wrote a few lines in Bengali to summarize the star-crossed lovers' situation:

> The blue of the sky fell in love with the green of the earth.
> The breeze between them sighs, "Alas!"

Proximity to Huiyin without the possibility of romance sent Xu into a state of deep frustration and sadness. He found solace in his friendship with Tagore. In a show of deep affection, Tagore had given his new friend a Bengali moniker, Susima, the name of an Indian prince. Xu called Tagore Rubidada, a playful version of "elder brother."

But the joy of the Asian brotherhood tour was not to last. Young radicals of the rising Communist Party and other political factions began to protest against Tagore's lectures, suggesting that the poet was living in the "world of the past." Communist Party leader Qu Qiubai declared that Tagore "still dreams that the message of 'love and light' can win over the heart of the English capitalist class. So he tries hard to ignore India's political struggle. India has already become modern India, but Tagore still seems to want to return to the abode of Brahma. No wonder he and India are moving in opposite directions—he has already retrogressed several hundred years."

Xu was deeply wounded by the anti-Tagore rhetoric, and for good reason. Before Tagore had decided to accept the invitation to tour China, Xu had worked hard to convince him to come. He had written Tagore assuring him of the country's political stability, the physical ease of the tour, and the "yearning" Chinese youths felt for the Indian poet's wisdom. But once Tagore began to lecture, he faced hostility from radical students throughout China.

Xu felt compelled to take the stage in defense of his new Indian mentor. On May 12, 1924, before Tagore delivered his last lecture in Beijing, Xu spoke to a large group of students about Tagore's pure intentions in visiting China and his love for the country:

> Fellow students, believe my words. A voice as great as [Tagore's] perhaps we shall never hear in our life again. . . . His personality can only find parallels in history. His magnanimous and tender soul, I am confident, will forever be a miracle in human memory. His infinite imagination and wide sympathy remind us of Whitman. His gospel of love and his zeal to promote it reminds us of Tolstoy. His strong will power and artistic talents remind us of Michelangelo, who created the statue of Moses. His humor and wisdom remind us of Socrates and Lao Tzu. The harmony and grace of his personality remind us of Goethe in his old age. His hands (whose touch conveys benevolence and pure love), his persistent work for humanity and his great and far-reaching voice sometimes invoke from us the image of the Savior; his radiance, his music and sublimity make us think of the great gods of Olympia.

Yet, despite Xu's efforts, the opposition to Tagore's presence in China grew even more heated. Soon after this Beijing speech, Tagore decided to cut his trip short. He gave his farewell lecture in Shanghai in front of some two thousand people, and on June 29 he and Xu left for a short visit to Japan. Three weeks later Xu returned to China, while Tagore journeyed back to India.

Tagore's visit to China marked a complex period for Xu. During Tagore's tour, Xu swung between profound happiness and heartache—dual forces that shaped so much of his adulthood. On one hand, he gained enormous renown from his work with Tagore; in addition, he developed a hugely influential relationship with the Indian poet-philosopher. On the other hand, he drew harsh criticism from the Chinese Communist Party for his alliance with Tagore and experienced heartbreak from the savage reactions to Tagore's messages of love and brotherhood.

On a personal level, Xu also experienced extreme moods brought on by the circumstances of the tour. While he was able to spend a prolonged period of time with Huiyin, she chose to remain aloof throughout. Thus, the woman who philosophically embodied what he believed about love and beauty was as distant to him as the stars.

RABINDRANATH TAGORE

(MAY 7, 1861–AUGUST 7, 1941)

Rabindranath Tagore is regarded as one of the greatest writers in modern Indian literature. A poet, novelist, painter, and educator, in 1913 he became the first non-European to win the Nobel Prize in Literature, primarily for his work *Gitanjali*, a collection of song offerings.

Tagore was born in Kolkata, India, to a prominent Brahmin family. His grandfather had established a huge financial empire and financed many public projects. The Tagore family members were pioneers of the Bengal Renaissance, a revival of the positive aspects of India's past and a celebration of the impact of modern Western ideas. Tagore was the youngest of fourteen children. His father, Maharishi Debendranath Tagore, was a spiritual teacher who was often away on pilgrimages to holy sites, and his mother, Sarada Devi, died when he was young. As a result, he was frequently lonely as a child and began writing poetry at the age of eight. He received his education from tutors and then at a variety of schools. Among these were the Bengal Academy, where he studied Bengali history and culture, and University College London, where he studied law, though he left after only one year there.

He published his first notable collection of poetry, *Manasi* or *The Ideal One*, in 1890. By the age of thirty, Tagore was already a famous poet. Yet he had within him the desire to accomplish more. He wanted to create an environment in which one could cultivate a feeling of interconnectedness with nature and all existence. He disliked formal education and instead believed that cultivating curiosity was the true path to intellectual discovery.

In 1901 he moved to Santiniketan, a family plot of land just outside Kolkata that was renamed to mean "abode of peace," to found an ashram and experimental school. Up until that point Tagore had spent the entirety of his life in Kolkata where he led a privileged existence. In Santiniketan, located in the hinterlands of Bengal, his eyes were opened to the difficulties of village life. He became intensely interested in the rural people who lived there. The experience humbled him and made him ashamed of his wealthy family's landlord status.

During this period in India, the professional classes of English-educated Indians began abandoning the countryside for the cities and with it their traditional duties to provide for the community. Tagore wanted to find a way to educate rural villagers and help lift them from poverty of both the mind and material life. His hope was that Santiniketan would become a connecting thread between India and the greater world and a place for studying humanity beyond the limits of nations and geography.

Though initially received harshly by critics, Tagore was eventually lauded for modernizing Bengali literature through his unorthodox, colloquial writing style. Between 1878 and 1932 he traveled as a lecturer to more than thirty countries on five continents. His travels included several stops in China, first in 1924, which is when he first met Xu Zhimo. The pair shared similar life philosophies and a passion for poetry, and they remained close friends for the remainder of Xu's life.

In addition to poetry, Tagore wrote novels, most famous among them *The Home and the World*, *Gora*, *Chokher Bhali*, and *The Gardener*. He also penned essays, short stories, travelogues, plays, and thousands of songs, in addition to writing the national anthems for both India and Bangladesh. At age sixty-three he took up painting and eventually created more than two thousand artworks. Tagore died at the age of eighty after many years of declining health. His legacy has long succeeded him—his poetry and good works are still revered by rich and poor in South Asia to this day.

CHAPTER SEVEN

A LITERARY
LOVE AND LIFE
IN CHINA

1924–1925

A QUEST FOR LOVE LEADS TO A GLAMOROUS SOCIALITE

Although Xu ached over the loss of Huiyin, he gradually began to accept romantic defeat. In fact, by the time of Tagore's tour, another young woman named Lu Xiaoman had caught his eye.

Xiaoman was married when she and Xu first met. Xu first came to know of her through her husband, Wang Geng, a fellow student of Liang Qichao's. Wang, who was often preoccupied by his work as a police chief in Harbin, invited Xu to accompany his vivacious wife to cultural events.

Xiaoman's father was Lu Ding, a government official who ensured that his only daughter, who was six years younger than Xu, received an excellent education. As a child, she attended Sacred Heart School, a private institution run by

Lu Xiaoman, artist, writer, ballroom dancer,
and socialite, at her desk.

French Catholic missionaries. At the same time, her parents arranged for her to be tutored in English by a British woman. By her mid-teens, she had an impressive command of both French and English. She was lauded for her beauty, quick mind, and talents as a performer. She could sing Peking opera arias to an almost professional standard and she fluidly danced the Western ballroom style. Later in her life she showed herself to be a talented painter and writer. When the Foreign Ministry of the Chinese government hosted dancing parties, she was a favored guest; social historians have noted that if Xiaoman did not appear at a high-level social event, crowds were disappointed.

As a result of her talents and social standing, many of Beijing's most elite families vied to arrange a marriage between her and their sons. A popular joke among them was that Xiaoman's hand was so in demand that the city's match-makers had worn out the threshold in front of her house.

After careful scrutiny of a long list of suitors, Xiaoman's parents had made a choice: she would marry Wang Geng, a handsome, accomplished young man born in 1895 to a wealthy family from Jiangsu Province. Like Xu, he was part of a wave of elite Chinese who traveled abroad for higher studies. He had attended the University of Michigan and Columbia University, transferring to Princeton University, from which he received his baccalaureate in 1915. He then attended the United States Military Academy at West Point (the future American president Dwight D. Eisenhower was enrolled at roughly the same time) and graduated with distinction. He spoke English, French, and German fluently.

In what was referred to as a "lightning marriage," Xiaoman and Wang wed within a month of their parents' agreement. The wedding ceremony, held at the Navy Club, was lauded as one of the notable Beijing social events of 1920. Wang was deeply devoted to his work, which left him little time to spend with his wife. This proved an essential point of contention between the pair, as Xiaoman thrived on going out and enjoying herself. It was in the interest of keeping his young wife happy that Wang began inviting Xu into his home. He often said to his wife, "Let Zhimo go with you."

With his wit, charisma, and easygoing demeanor, Xu was the ideal social partner for Xiaoman. On weekends, Wang would take his wife out to the Grand Hotel des Wagons-Lits to dance, to the theater for Peking opera, or for a stroll around the West Hills. But on weekdays, Wang invited Xu to take his place. Before long, Xu and Xiaoman were deeply in love.

THE CRESCENT MOON SOCIETY

The small production of *Chitra*, which Xu and Huiyin took part in during Tagore's tour, coupled with his knowledge and experience of the Bloomsbury Group, inspired the young poet to organize more cultural gatherings and events for his lively group of Chinese intelligentsia. In the late summer of 1923, he founded an informal dining club that included Beijing's cultural elite, as well as a number of bankers and politicians interested in the arts. In time Xu would name this club the Crescent Moon Society, drawing from Tagore's 1913 book of poems, *Crescent Moon*. The group took up residence at No. 7 Center Street in Beijing, and there, members could sup together and play billiards and other social games. The modest monthly dues included biweekly dinners and some form of planned entertainment.

However, with Xu managing the enterprise, much went awry. He did not create a formal membership list, nor did he collect dues. The biweekly dinners never materialized with any regularity, although Xiaoman once performed an after-dinner play, *A Nun Longs for a Secular World*. Some biographers theorize that Xu created the Crescent Moon Society as a response to his rebuff by Huiyin. The club allowed him to emerge from his social isolation, stand at the center of an exchange of cultural ideas, and meet interesting people with whom he could forge a new future.

THE TEST OF A NEW LOVE

By early 1925 Xu and Xiaoman had taken up their affair wholeheartedly. Their obvious passion for each other generated much gossip among Beijing society, as well as disapproval among their friends and family. When Wang Geng finally realized the gravity of the relationship, he banned the poet from his house and instructed Xiaoman to spend more time at home. This painful situation compelled the poet to speak out against traditional morality in China, stating that people who could not sympathize with his and Xiaoman's plight of star-crossed love were creatures "whose blood vessels were filled with icy cold water." According to Youyi's memoir, Wang threatened to have Xu killed, which caused the poet profound embarrassment. At that point, like many a thwarted lover, Xu decided he needed to take a break from Xiaoman and China.

Xu decided to embark on what he would call a "sentimental journey," a term that would obscure his real reasons for leaving: to reflect on and test his relationship with Xiaoman. Instead, Xu wished to focus the trip on completing his education, clearing his mind, meeting Tagore in Europe, visiting with European authors, and paying his respects at the graves of other notable writers.

Before leaving China, he coaxed a few Wang family servants to deliver letters, three in all, to Xiaoman. In one such missive he asked her to keep a daily diary in lieu of writing him letters. He also urged her to approach their separation and the turmoil with her husband and family courageously. Finally, he reassured her of his devotion. He wrote that he treasured her love.

In this excerpt from one of those March 1925 letters, one can sense Xu's commitment to the new woman in his life and the force of his convictions, as well as his social naiveté:

> A rare and wonderful flower like you most certainly is not to be sacrificed to a pair of parents and a husband lacking in understanding. You are responsible to God, to your newly discovered love. . . . Even if fate dictates that you encounter unavoidable death before achieving final victory . . . then die, for such death is success and victory.

In his third letter, dated March 10, he wrote about the depth of his feelings for Xiaoman:

> My dear Little Dragon, haven't you already promised to be my eternal companion? I can no longer let go of you, my dear heart. You are mine. You are my sole achievement in life. . . . You are my life, my poetry; you are entirely mine. . . . If you say as much as half of a "No," then let a thunderbolt strike me dead and end it all.

CHAPTER EIGHT

A SENTIMENTAL JOURNEY THROUGH EUROPE

1925

THE DEATH OF A SON

On March 11, after writing his letters to Xiaoman, Xu took the Trans-Siberian Railway to Europe. His first stop was in Moscow, where he exchanged telegrams with his former wife, Youyi, still living in Germany. He discovered that his youngest son, Peter, then three, had died of peritonitis less than a week earlier. Flooded with remorse, he wrote a memorial essay for his dead child:

Peter, my dear Peter. . . .

You shall never be able to hear these words, yet through mourning you, I wanted to somehow give vent to my suppressed emotions. In this unnatural world, there are many other people in my similar, or even worse, condition and experience. Perhaps these are people who will listen to what I want to say, and will have sympathy for me.

The Ponte Vecchio Bridge in Florence, the city that inspired Xu's 1925 poem "A Night in Florence," the title work of his second volume of poetry.

Say, for example, your mother, Peter; did she ever have a single day of happiness and joy? Nevertheless, in her equally miserable condition, she showed wisdom, patience, and more impressively, courage and determination. At least she, I daresay, will understand the nuances of my words. . . .

Peter, you came to this mortal world as if a guest, only for a short stay. What you knew was the love from your kind mother, the warmth of the sunshine, the prettiness of the flowers and the grass. When you left your mother's bosom, you returned to the embrace of God. And I am sure he is now listening joyfully to the report of your stay on this earth. . . . Your little feet were never touched by those merciless thorns, and the white clothes you wore when you came were never stained by the mud.

Decades later, in her memoir, Youyi remarked of this memorial letter: "This sounds like a man who cares very much about family and takes responsibilities. . . . But judging from his actions, I do not think he worried about whether we had enough money or how we lived. You see, that is the way it is with the artist."

SEEKING LITERARY RENEWAL

The death of Xu's son left him emotionally depleted, but he willed himself to carry on with his journey. During his travels through Russia, Italy, France, and England, he visited the graves of Anton Chekhov, Peter Kropotkin, Katherine Mansfield, Voltaire, Victor Hugo, Keats, and Shelley. Xu later said that he embarked on his trip in part to indulge in hero worship of these revered members of the literati.

In England, Goldsworthy Lowes Dickinson wrote a letter of introduction for his protégé to Thomas Hardy. The author, almost eighty-three at the time, rarely accepted guests, but Dickinson had told him that Xu had translated several of his poems into Chinese, which intrigued Hardy. During their visit, Hardy questioned the young poet about Chinese poetry and language: Did the Chinese use rhyme? Was the Chinese language too difficult to learn to be practical?

Before Xu departed, Hardy took him to his garden, where he plucked a small bouquet of flowers and handed them to his visitor as a memento.

On that same day, Xu visited Exeter Cathedral and wrote the poem "In Front of Exeter Cathedral," in which the poet asks the old religious edifice, "Who is responsible for the strange course of human life?" The answer comes to the writer in various forms: from a star overhead that gives him a "wink"; from the cathedral that has grown "tired of watching such tragicomedies" of human life; and from a nearby tree that allows its "mottled leaves" to fall near the poet's feet.

While on his journey, Xu also invited Youyi to join him on a trip to Italy. She agreed, if only to take a much-needed break from her life as a teacher in Berlin, and to alleviate the grief she felt at the loss of Peter. The journey together was not meant as a reconciliation; in fact, two English friends accompanied the former couple on their travels.

During the tour, Xu grew enamored of Florence. Away from the distractions Xiaoman presented, he wrote freely in the Italian city, which became one of his favorite places. "A Night in Florence," which he composed at this time, became the title work of his second volume of poetry.

In Florence, Youyi recalled, Xu once again began to act in quite a peculiar manner. He started evading her, just as he had in Sawston when he was trying to conceal his relationship with Huiyin, and at breakfast each morning he would wait impatiently for a letter or telegram from his friend Hu Shi in China. As it turned out, Xu was looking for communication from China about when it would be safe to return. One morning about five months into his European travels, Xu looked up from a letter and said, "Good, we can leave now." According to Youyi's memoir, Hu Shi had let him know that Xiaoman's husband, Wang Geng, no longer wanted to have Xu killed. The poet was finally clear to go home.

ZHANG YOUYI

Zhang Youyi may have begun her adult life as a young bride without a high level of education, but she ultimately rose to become a cosmopolitan woman of impressive achievements. This is despite the fact that her divorce, reputedly the first legal marriage dissolution in Chinese history, forced her to accept a life completely different from that of Chinese women in the past. Without substantial financial support from her husband or family, she took on the challenges of single motherhood with courage and a remarkable sense of independence.

It is interesting to note that while her former husband, Xu Zhimo, doggedly chased that which was modern, Youyi instead made quiet decisions that manifested her progressive thinking. By the end of her life, she was by all measures a highly accomplished, self-made woman of the twentieth century, even against all the odds she had faced.

Youyi's life took place against a backdrop of great change in China, and in many ways her course can be seen as a reflection of this social, political, and cultural flux. She was born in 1900, the eighth of twelve children, and the second daughter, born to a widely respected doctor and his aristocratic wife. When Youyi turned three, her mother began the excruciatingly painful process of breaking and binding her daughter's feet (a centuries-old tradition that was a symbol of class and refinement). However, when Youyi screamed in pain, her brother begged their mother to spare the young girl. As a result, Youyi became the first daughter in her family to escape the mutilation that had maimed and immobilized generations of women—the family's first major step, so to speak, toward modernity.

As a teen, Youyi pestered her parents to send her to boarding school near Shanghai, even though they did not think educating girls was necessary. They acquiesced when Youyi pointed out that the institution's fees were so affordable that it would cost less for her to be at school than at home. "Where my desire to study came from I do not know," Youyi told her grandniece Pang-Mei Natasha Chang, to whom Youyi dictated her 1996 memoir, *Bound Feet & Western Dress*. "In Mama's day, a woman never left the inner chambers of her quarters until

Youyi in the early 1930s.

she took leave of her father's house to marry. . . . It was unthinkable for a girl to pursue learning outside the home." Looking back at that period, Youyi believed her desire to learn came from knowing she "had been born into changing times." Her well-educated brothers also inspired her perspective and admiration.

Youyi had to leave school at fifteen when she was summoned to marry Xu Zhimo, then eighteen, a situation that saddened her. However, her intention to remain a dutiful daughter took precedence over her desires for an education. As it would turn out, these few years of formal education would serve her well. After she and Xu divorced in 1922, Youyi, then twenty-two and alone with a newborn, studied childhood education at the Pestalozzi-Fröbel-Haus in Berlin to become a kindergarten teacher. In the process, she developed a strong command of German and English. In the years to come, she would also study Japanese.

After living in Europe independently for four years, Youyi returned to China as a twenty-six-year-old divorcee, at a time when such a legal dissolution of marriage brought with it a serious social stigma. Yet she was able to found the popular Shanghai-based Yunchang (Clouds and Clothing) boutique. She also assumed the position of vice president of Shanghai Women's Savings Bank, the first female to do so. As an independent woman, she flourished.

Even after her marriage dissolved, Youyi demonstrated her character through her actions, maintaining her connection to Xu's family; her familial love and her sense of responsibility to them remained. She often supported Xu, custom-ordering clothes for him and, on occasion, offering him financial help. Following her divorce, she continued to care for her ex-husband's parents. With money she made on the Shanghai stock market, she built a home next to her own for her former in-laws. For years after Xu Zhimo died, Youyi went as far as depositing monthly funds in Lu Xiaoman's bank account. "I felt it was my son's duty to provide for her," she told her biographer.

When her son Jikai and his wife left for studies in America, Youyi took on raising his four children. In 1949, when Mao Zedong declared the creation of the People's Republic of China, Youyi escaped the political turmoil by fleeing with her grandchildren across the border, first to

Macau and then to Hong Kong. There, she cared for the children on her own for three years and became a mother figure to them. When the time came for Youyi to send her grandchildren to the United States, she sat them down on her bed in her Hong Kong apartment and spoke with them about their future and their reunion with their father and mother.

"You may feel as though your parents are strangers, but you will enjoy being with them in America," she said, reaching out to gently touch the hands of each of her young charges. She did not once mention to her grandchildren the loneliness she would face without them. As it turned out, immigration issues would keep Youyi from moving to the States for several decades.

In 1954 Youyi married Su Jizhi, a Hong Kong doctor. She not only helped him keep track of his medical appointments and financial books but also convinced him to stop drinking, which was interfering with his family relationships. She took her second husband back to Cam-

Tony Hsu as a young boy with his sisters (from left to right) Margaret, Angela, and Fern with grandmother Zhang Youyi in their garden in Shanghai's French Concession, 1947. Soon after this photograph was taken, the family would leave China for a new life in Hong Kong.

bridge, where she visited her old Sawston cottage and sat on the banks of the Cam, just as Xu Zhimo had done many decades before. "I realized how beautiful Cambridge was, I had never known that before," she told her biographer.

After revisiting the cities she had shared with Xu, Youyi realized she wanted to compile all of the poet's work into an anthology, *The Complete Works of Xu Zhimo,* published in Taiwan in 1958.

Youyi spent her years in Hong Kong donating her time and resources to many charities, among them programs for underprivileged children. Her grown grandchildren visited, and as they walked down the city streets with her, they marveled at the many people who stopped to thank her for her wide-ranging altruistic work and many acts of kindness. After her second husband died, Youyi moved to New York and spent her final years with her son and grandchildren.

The dramatic scope of her life was explored in detail in *Bound Feet.* The much-lauded book, which received international attention, transformed Youyi into a symbol of female self-empowerment. Youyi died in 1989, seven years before her memoir was published. She is buried next to her son Jikai and her daughter-in-law in Westchester, New York.

CHAPTER NINE

AGAINST THE ODDS, LOVE PREVAILS

1925–1927

A NEW LIFE WITH XIAOMAN

While Xu was traveling in Europe, Xiaoman was battling tremendous pressure from her husband and parents. In July 1925 she tried to end the affair with Xu, asking him to return to China so she could bid him farewell. In her passionate letter to him she wrote:

> All that happened before between us, a brief period of happiness, can only be regarded as a spring dream, an illusory shadow, that leaves no trace to be treasured in memory. . . .Why did the Lord of Heaven create you and me? Why does He make it impossible for us to be together? Now the only hope I have is to see you once more upon your return so that I can tell you everything that has been concealed in my heart during these several months. . . . The romance between you and me will end right here. . . . From now on, don't hanker after me anymore. You are a person with hopes,

Xu and Xiaoman wed in Beihai Gardens in Beijing, October 3, 1926. Both fought hard for their right to divorce their first spouses and marry each other, but the lightness of their wedding day was not to last.

and your future is much brighter than mine. You mustn't ruin it because of me. I am not worthy of your pity. . . . Don't feel bad, but only remember that the person leaving you is not I, for I will be in your heart night and day.

Both Wang Geng and Xiaoman's parents demanded that Xiaoman leave Beijing to join her husband at his new post as the chief of staff for the warlord General Sun Quanfang in Nanjing. Instead, she made an abrupt emotional turn and decided to head to Shanghai to divorce Wang. On September 5, 1925, Xu landed in Shanghai and continued directly onward to Xiashi, his hometown, to see his parents and await news of Xiaoman's divorce.

Wang Geng became increasingly philosophical about the failure of his marriage and finally consented to grant Xiaoman a divorce. "Marriage is a matter between husband and wife," he wrote in a letter to her. "As long as they get along well, they stay married; otherwise they ought to separate. Since we have had a friendly relationship as husband and wife, let us from now on be friends." His parting message also included a warning to Xu: if the poet were ever to mistreat Xiaoman, he declared, there would be consequences.

Even with Wang's consent, Xu found that his path to marrying Xiaoman was hardly unobstructed. Neither Xiaoman's family nor his own parents were in favor of the union. Indeed, Xiaoman's mother—fearing that Xu was still legally married, meaning that her daughter would have the lowly status of a concubine or second wife—insisted he would have to go through his entire divorce proceeding with Youyi again in China.

As a solution, Xu and his parents arranged for Youyi to return home to confirm that they had indeed gone through with the legal parting. Youyi recalls in her memoir that she met the Xus and their son at a Shanghai hotel. She noticed that Xu was wearing an expensive dark-green jade ring. Xu's father asked her, "Is it true that you and my son have divorced?" When she confirmed the split, the Xus looked deeply dismayed; they had hoped Youyi would object to the divorce and remain part of their family.

They then asked her the question that would forever alter Xu's life: "Do you have any objection to Lu Xiaoman?" When Youyi shook her head no, Xu leapt from his chair and cried out, flinging his arms wide in joy—and his jade ring flew out an open window. Xu's expression of jubilation became one of horror: the ring had been Xiaoman's engagement present to him. The entire Xu family searched the lawn, but the ring was never found. Youyi later said that she felt this incident was a bad omen for his marriage to Xiaoman.

Xu's parents could not forbid the marriage, but they laid down strict conditions for it. First of all, they would not pay for the ceremony. Xu himself would have to raise the funds for his wedding. Furthermore, they stipulated that Liang Qichao would have to serve as witness at the wedding, a way of giving the Xu family face. Lastly, after they were married, Xu and his new wife would have to live in the family compound in Xiashi. Xu and Xiaoman agreed to all of these demands.

Professionally, this period of his life brought a series of significant achievements for Xu. During August of that same year he published his first book of poetry, *Poems of Zhimo*, which introduced Western rhymes, meters, and themes to Chinese literature. It was an immediate success, and he was lauded as a hugely promising poet. Coupled with his success as Tagore's interpreter and a popular essayist and translator of such Western authors as Hardy and Mansfield, Xu had become a national celebrity. Now, with his imminent marriage to Xiaoman, a glamorous and charismatic woman he loved wholly and passionately, it seemed his life, and his ideals, could finally take flight.

In August 1926, two days after Chiang Kai-shek and the Kuomintang entered Changsha, the capital of Hunan Province, as part of the Nationalist Party's Northern Expedition (a military campaign to reunify China), Xu held a lavish party in Beijing to celebrate his upcoming wedding to Xiaoman. Having struggled for years and bearing intense pressure from their families and society, they were finally able to live together as husband and wife. They had not only their love to honor but also their creative work: love letters, poems to each other, unflinchingly honest diaries—all of which they would soon publish. Xu felt that he had found his "soul's companion." Indeed, even this new love's name was auspicious: Xiaoman's first name included one of the same characters as Katherine Mansfield's Chinese name. The pair felt they had much to celebrate. Yet the truth of the matter was that parties such as this would mark the beginning of the couple's fast spiral into overwhelming debt.

XU'S SECOND MARRIAGE: BEAUTIFUL CLOUDS AND HARD RAIN

On October 3, 1926, Xu and Xiaoman were married in Beijing in Beihai Park. Perhaps in the spirit of modernity, Xu had invited Youyi to his wedding. She did not attend, nor did his parents. Liang Qichao acted as the master of ceremonies and was slated to give the wedding speech. However, in his address, instead of celebrating this fusion of souls, Liang delivered a shocking diatribe against the couple.

To Xu he said, "By nature you are restless, and therefore, academically, you have no achievement. As you are fickle-minded, you have divorced your wife and are now marrying again. . . . From now on you must thoroughly rectify your past mistakes and lead a new life." He then gave the couple a joint reprimand, repeating his strongest sentiments: "Both of you have had a divorce and are marrying for the second time, all due to your fickle-mindedness. Hereafter you must deeply repent. . . . Congratulations to you both for this, your last marriage." The following day Liang wrote about the Xu-Lu wedding to his daughter:

> The youth make such a thing of love; they show no sense of moderation, but arbitrarily smash through the protective nets of convention, and so fall into their own sorrowful snare. This is so very pitiable. Xu Zhimo is really intelligent; I love him; even though I saw him on this occasion sink so far beyond his depth, yet I never lost hope that I could extricate him from the predicament.

> Another thing that upsets me deeply is that all his old friends are profoundly disgusted by his behavior. If he insists on behaving like this and is then rejected by society, that will be his decision. . . . Yet when I look at him I am filled with such pity for him, and worry that this is the kind of situation that leads to suicide.

Xu saw the situation in entirely different terms. Soon after his wedding, he wrote to his English friend Leonard Elmhirst: "I triumphed against the deadly force of ignorance and prejudice in which all societies rest."

This triumph would prove to be a momentary one.

After the wedding, Xu traveled with his bride from Beijing to Shanghai, where they lived in a humble hotel. At the time, the Xu family was constructing a new compound in Xiashi to accommodate the couple. Once the work was completed, Xu and Xiaoman descended upon the groom's home village, but not without a grand show of drama. Youyi told her biographer that Xiaoman had demanded a red bridal chair instead of an everyday palanquin to bring her to the compound for the first time. It was an extravagance that required eight hired hands to carry the chair, as opposed to the usual two. This was not the only issue to disrupt the household. Youyi's in-laws complained that from the first night, Xiaoman would only eat half a bowl of rice, an act that was seen as a cultural insult. Rice, after all, was the food of the country; the grains had to be painstakingly cultivated, tilled, and husked. Leaving a grain of rice behind was like failing to appreciate the bead of sweat dripping from the rice farmer's brow. That same night, Xiaoman asked her new husband to carry her up a long, steep flight of stairs, appropriating the Western tradition of a bride's crossing the threshold in her husband's arms. The Xus considered their new daughter-in-law to be frivolous and lazy. They decided to leave the house, and Xu's father took a train out of the village soon after Xiaoman's arrival.

Scholars believe that Xu returned to his family home for several reasons, among them being his intentions to redeem himself as a son, offer his bride the opportunity to learn domestic skills, and, on a more practical level, take advantage of the food and lodging his parents provided. The situation immediately imploded, not only because his parents disliked Xiaoman but also because civil unrest was making it more and more dangerous to live in the countryside. They also felt deeply the loss of their former daughter-in-law, Youyi, whose sensible, dutiful behavior they admired. Despite her divorce from their son, the Xus still loved and depended upon her and considered her a close relative. In fact, they would later live with Youyi, who set up house in Shanghai.

Xu Zhimo decided to decamp with his new wife to Shanghai, only to discover that he could draw no more than a limited allowance from his father's bank account. He had to take a loan from his uncle before he could so much as travel. Thus began Xu's fraught relationship with money.

Shanghai, considered the most cosmopolitan city in Asia at the time, was a port whose waterfront boulevard, the Bund, sparkled with grand colonial buildings and skyscrapers. *Time* magazine described 1920s Shanghai as an "exotic stew of Jewish opium traders, Chinese compradors and Viennese dancing girls." In 1926 Aldous Huxley wrote about the densely populated, wild, and glamorous city: "Yes, it will all be there, just as intensely and tenaciously alive as ever—all there a thousand years hence, five thousand, ten. You have only to stroll through Shanghai to be certain of it. London and Paris offer no such certainty."

In Shanghai, Xiaoman, who had been raised in an upper-class household and was welcomed into the highest levels of society when she lived in Beijing, had little interest in economizing, even if her new financial status with Xu called for frugality. Instead, she reveled in nights spent dancing and enjoying theater. Xu's diary entry on December 27, 1926, shows him complaining about foiled plans: he had been hoping to go to a church to sing Christmas carols, but Xiaoman insisted that they instead perform in a Chinese opera and dance at a commercial ballroom. "I wanted on a winter night with heavy frost and pale moonbeam to write a few lines of poetry that stemmed from the warmth of my soul, but instead I had to follow the crowd to a dancing hall with a well-waxed floor to admire the female dancers' gleaming shoes and stockings."

Shanghai was a world completely different from both his beloved Cambridge and his home in Xiashi. The city's noise, traffic, and tall buildings, coupled with Xiaoman's health, which had always been delicate, and their relatively tight quarters made for a depressing existence. For both husband and wife, their new position as have-nots—at least in comparison to the upper-crust friends that surrounded them—must have made them feel like orphaned children standing in front of a gleaming restaurant window while plates of steaming dumplings and jasmine tea were served to patrons. During this period, Xu made these revealing entries in his journals:

The past is a heap of ashes, thoroughly burnt, not a word left.

Terribly bored; finishing three glasses of brandy.

Time was spent in boredom. Meaningless; cold; the same everywhere.

Xu had most likely begun to question his marriage to Xiaoman. In a letter dated April 1, 1927, the poet wrote to Leonard Elmhirst about his wife: "She is a naughty kid that still needs badly looking after." He could no longer deny that his young wife, six years his junior, was a flamboyant spendthrift who enjoyed the glamorous life, while he, on the other hand, was an intellectual who preferred to pursue a more reflective path. In addition, in choosing Xiaoman, the poet had alienated his parents, to whom he had always been devoted. Perhaps most importantly, his union with Xiaoman did not inspire any significant writing.

Despite their differences, Xu was always careful to conceal his frustrations, never pointing to Xiaoman as the cause of any emotional, creative, or financial despair—a reflection of his character and his pride. He had positioned himself as an idealist who would sacrifice in order to unite with the woman he loved.

When he had declared he would divorce his first wife, Youyi, it was in the name of fighting a cultural anachronism—arranged marriage. However, once he was free to choose Xiaoman as his lifelong partner, this free will did not bring him the happiness or romance he had idealized. In obscuring his marital issues in his writings and conversations, Xu showed a deep concern with saving face and maintaining a noble image.

While in England, Xu had read the Irish critic and poet Edward Dowden's *The Life of Robert Browning* and been impressed by the romance and literary partnership of the Brownings. Clearly, after his love affair with Huiyin imploded, he set his sights on Xiaoman to realize the dream of such a relationship. Their early letters and journal entries written for each other showed a high level of promise and reflected Xu's ambitions for their marriage:

> We are people of high minds and must not slacken in the least. We must set an upright, genuine example. . . . We now have a small number of friends who as far as intellectual excellence is concerned are the elite in China. They love us genuinely, rate us highly and expect a great deal from us. They are anxious to see us achieve something beyond the attainment of average men and realize the world which ordinary people can only dream of. They, I am confident, believe you and I have the necessary natural endowments and abilities. . . . So for ourselves, for our friends, for society, for Heaven, we shoulder a responsibility that requires us to struggle to the end—for absolute perfection.

Xiaoman's allure was obvious to everyone who met her, even to Youyi, who had dinner with the younger woman once at the request of Xu's close friend Hu Shi. At the dinner table that night, Youyi said, she "realized just how beautiful Lu Xiaoman was. Her skin was lustrous and her features very fine. All the men were captivated when she spoke." Throughout the meal she witnessed Xiaoman's coquettish interplay with her former husband. "She called Zhimo 'Mo Mo' and he called her 'Man'—an endearment of Xiaoman. He spoke to her with such patience, such respect. All of this I observed and remembered that, with me, Xu Zhimo had always been curt."

THE SCRAMBLE TO SURVIVE

While she clearly had many charms, Xiaoman also had a flighty quality to her personality, forever flitting toward the shiny and beautiful. This characteristic would undermine all of Xu's hopes for a literary partnership and would prove to be the marriage's undoing, the death of Xu's ideal.

Xiaoman had long suffered from an erratic heartbeat and fatigue, and her strenuous performance schedule would leave her further depleted. In the spring of 1927, after seven months of marriage, she became acquainted with an amateur actor, Weng Ruiwu, originally from Anhui Province. He, too, was descended from a highborn and cultured family. His father, a provincial officer in the Qing bureaucracy, was also a famous painter and collector of rare paintings. Weng was lauded in Shanghai for his operatic and acting abilities, and he and Xiaoman sang leading roles alongside each other on many occasions. By the time the two had starred in a couple of plays together, they had become close friends, and Xu welcomed Weng into his home.

One particularly strenuous performance left Xiaoman bedridden. Weng, who had mastered a form of therapeutic massage, offered his services. Xiaoman proclaimed that the treatment was healing her, so Xu did not question the arrangement. What the poet did not realize was that Weng and Xiaoman had quickly become romantically involved. Weng also introduced Xiaoman to opium smoking, claiming that it would aid her circulation and cure her fatigue. After a number of smoking sessions, Xiaoman had become an opium addict.

Opium, a highly addictive narcotic derived from the pods of unripe opium poppy, wreaked havoc on all levels of Chinese society. The use of the drug caused a widespread and devastating chemical dependency that raged through China in the nineteenth and early twentieth centuries. Photographs from the period show the drug's catastrophic effects throughout the Middle Kingdom: dozens of Chinese lying side by side on mats, inhaling from pipes, bodies limp, eyes glazed, faces gaunt. Opium left its users in a mental haze, their vision blurred, and their bodies withering as the drug decimated their appetite. It was believed that even rats became addicted and gathered on the rafters whenever an opium hookah was lit.

The daily smoking of the drug not only lulled Xiaoman into a dreamlike state but also sapped her creative energy and talent and ravaged her beauty. This addiction bonded her to Weng, who shared the pipe with her for hours each day.

Xu's parents, who now spent much of their time in Shanghai, witnessed Xiaoman's opium use, and at one point during these difficult years, they called Youyi, who had settled in Shanghai, in a state of intense anger. Xu's mother claimed that Xiaoman had begun to demand certain foods for Weng and spent most of her days lying next to the actor on an opium bed, sharing the pipe. One night, in fact, Xu himself had come home from his job teaching literature at a university to find the pair curled up on the opium bed. Still hoping to be with Xiaoman, he lay next to her, with Weng on the other side. The next morning, his parents, who had come for a visit, found the trio sharing the one small bed, with Xu asleep but almost falling off the side. It was more than the Xu parents could tolerate.

"The family has come to ruin," Xu's mother cried to Youyi, signaling a distinct turning point in their relationship with a son whose judgment they could no longer respect.

At the same time, the Xu family was suffering significant financial setbacks as well. Their once flourishing enterprises and investments had atrophied; the country's raging civil wars made it difficult for the family to manage its many businesses. Xu's parents had already reduced their son's funding, and he found himself scrambling not only to pay for such basics as housing and food but also to support Xiaoman's love of fashionable clothing, her considerable doctor bills, and her all-consuming opium addiction. The poet fell into a depression, as reflected in his diary entry of April 20, 1927:

> In the morning, I can hardly stay awake, and when the nighttime comes, before I can do anything, I begin to feel drowsy. My mind is almost completely blank. . . . If I want to write poetry, I haven't a trace of poetic sentiment, let alone poetic lines. . . . I almost don't know how to keep my diary. . . . Recalling how I used to write poems and letters, I really feel that now I'm not up to my former self.

That same day Xiaoman encouraged her husband to write a poem. He wrote "The Last Days of Spring," a telling metaphor for his personal state. He ended the poem with these lines:

> At night a knell-like sound exhorts repeatedly:
> "The fresh blossoms in the vase of your life, too,
> Have changed their looks; who is there to bury their lovely remains?"

Desperate to keep afloat, Xu scrambled to secure teaching positions. As a professor at Kwang Hua University in Shanghai, he taught English translation and British literature. At the same time, at Soochow University, Xu's good friend John Wu secured him a position as an English professor. These two jobs brought in a decent base salary but certainly not enough to support his lifestyle with Xiaoman. He was forced to consider other ways to augment his earnings.

CHAPTER TEN

ART AND ENTERPRISE

1927–1928

THE POET FINDS HIS WAY

To Xu's credit, even though his father had lavishly supported him for most of his life, he took his new financial burdens seriously, always looking for ways he could use his talents and passions to develop new enterprises and business opportunities. A few years earlier, just after his return from his self-dubbed "sentimental journey," Xu had put his poetry-writing ambitions aside and taken on the editorship of the *Morning Post Literary Supplement* (also known as *Chenbao*) in Beijing. He assumed this role with authority and gravitas. In his debut address to readers, he took a staunch position. He would serve as an editor with a distinct perspective:

> I will not cater to the mentality of the masses; I will not flatter the authorities of public opinion; I will not ingratiate myself with society's dull stupidity and biased shallowness. I will try only to know myself and shoulder my own responsibilities. I will not say even under compulsion anything that I do not want to say, and will say anything I want to say despite pressure or entreaties. . . . I will serve as editor with full authority.

Xu visited Tagore in Santiniketan, India, on his return from Europe to China in 1928. He stayed in this house of Tagore's.

Beyond the promise of a regular paycheck, Xu saw in this editor's post an opportunity to develop modern Chinese poetry and the seriousness of his own literary contributions as well. As part of the *Supplement*, he launched the ambitious *Shikan Poetry Monthly*, calling for submissions and enlisting the editorial acumen of China's top scribes. In the editor's letter of the debut issue, Xu explained how the magazine sprang from a core group of poets who met regularly at the home of the writer Wen Yiduo. At such gatherings, each member spoke of his own poetic compositions and modern poetic theories and offered advice on how to move the genre forward. Xu was not a founding member of this particular group; in fact, he had to invite himself to the meetings, but in time, he became a core member.

The members, he wrote,

> share a common faith that poetry is an implement for the manifestation of human creative power, similar in terms to music and art. . . . Our responsibility is to discover for poetry . . . a new form and a new rhythm. We believe that a perfect form is the sole manifestation of a perfect spirit, and that the life of literature and art is the accomplishment of invisible inspiration plus conscious perseverance and painstaking effort. Finally, we believe that our new literature and art, just like our nation, will have a great and glorious future.

Although *Shikan Poetry Monthly* only published eleven issues, it had a lasting effect on the country's writers. Wen Yiduo and the other poets put forth the idea of creating a form and establishing a rhythm for modern Chinese poetry. Wen stressed the importance of rhythmic evenness, regularity of lines, metrical feet, and end rhymes. The Harvard-educated writer Liang Shiqiu observed that this was the first time in Chinese history that a collection of poets had gathered to create a new form of poetry with a distinct shared vision. During the short, glorious run of *Shikan Poetry Monthly*, all the poets involved wrote with these new parameters in mind. Even poets who had not previously considered modern structure began to experiment with the new rules. Of course, this perceived conformity inspired many writers to criticize the new trend, calling the new framework "square block poetry" and "dry bean curd squares poetry." But this did not deter a generation of up-and-coming writers from integrating the group's parameters into their own verses.

Meanwhile, in the northern part of the country, the political unrest in

The two poets shared a bond that would resonate through time.

Beijing had heightened, and **warlords** dominated the city. Many scholars and writers who found the turmoil unbearable fled Beijing and relocated to Shanghai, where Xu was based. He tapped into this new impressive concentration of literati and invited these writers to share in his efforts to move Chinese poetry forward, in particular in the creation of a publishing enterprise. To this end, he asked his growing circle of literary friends to buy shares in the venture and managed to raise a small amount of funds.

In 1927 Xu used this money to establish the Crescent Moon Bookstore. In September that year, Crescent Moon published Xu's second volume of poetry, *A Night in Florence*, which he had mostly written during his 1925 journey through Europe. Xu described the work as a "vestige of a relatively grave period of upheaval in his life," a time when he was struggling to unite with Xiaoman. He offered this book as a first anniversary present to his wife and wrote in the preface:

> Please accept this volume of poems as a modest present for the commemoration of our marriage. . . . Fortunately, your thoughts . . . are not centered on gold, pearls, and precious gems. These incomplete poetic lines are not worth a farthing, but in view of my dire poverty, the mere mention of which makes me blush, they can be considered the only savings I have been able to make during these last three years.

It is clear from this preface that Xu was still deeply in love with his wife and felt responsible for their challenging financial situation.

In addition to his editing and writing, he also generated income from his translations, including eight of Katherine Mansfield's short stories and Voltaire's *Candide*. The sales of *A Night in Florence* also somewhat buoyed the Xu household finances; in May 1928 Xu released his revised version of the collection. One reflection of Xu Zhimo's popularity as a poet is the fact that by 1933, *A Night in Florence* was in its sixth printing. Juggling all of these enterprises, Xu brought home a comfortable monthly salary.

And yet this was still not enough to support the couple at their former level of glory. Xiaoman's opium addiction had spun out of control. Not only did her fogged state of mind burden the household, Xu was also pushed to the borders of his marriage by Weng's presence. Xu's solution: to pour his attention into developing literary enterprises and find other ways to support their lifestyle.

XU'S CRESCENT MOON CLIQUE AND ITS DETRACTORS

Xu continued to develop several publishing enterprises in the late 1920s, many with the name Crescent Moon, as a way of cultivating his financial and career success. Several years prior, in 1924, the poet and his literary cronies had unofficially created the Crescent Moon Society, on that night in Beijing when Xu, Huiyin, and members of their circle had staged the play *Chitra* for Tagore. Riding on the triumph of that event, Xu capitalized on the name "Crescent Moon." He and his like-minded friends staged many other lively plays, musicals, and readings, and collaborated on various creative enterprises under that name. Drawn from one of Tagore's most famous poetry collections, Crescent Moon—along with its imagery and lyrical resonance—had inspired and fueled the group for years. As Xu would later write, "the new moon is not a powerful symbol. Nevertheless, its delicate arch shape clearly hints that it will embrace future fullness." By 1928 the society had mostly disbanded, but the eponymous book-publishing venture Crescent Moon Bookstore flourished, releasing Xu's work as well as that of his literary contemporaries.

On March 10, 1928, Xu and his friends published the first issue of the *Crescent Moon Monthly*, which the poet stressed was an entity separate from the society and the publishing company. The publication was the creation of this small, united group of literary compeers. They expressed that they had no formal organization or set points of conviction, except that they shared a few common ideals—the presentation of engaging ideas, vibrant, progressive writing, and a show of optimism in an era of great political turbulence. In the lead article of the *Monthly*'s debut issue, Xu wrote:

> It is a period of chaos in which all criteria of worth are topsy-turvy. In order to . . . eradicate all evil forces in order that the light of day be seen again, to dredge and regulate the source of the vital force, and to emancipate the irrepressible creative activities—such gigantic undertakings, of course, can be dreams.

He also emphasized that the creative forces behind the *Monthly* supported, rather than suppressed, freedom of opinion. And yet the country's leftist writers attacked the publication and called the founding literati and its frequent contributors "members of the Crescent Moon clique." The opponents of the magazine harped on the *Monthly*'s considerable influence, its social cachet, and its support of Western ideas and culture. Indeed, it was in the *Monthly* that Xu published many of his translations of English and Continental stories and essays—those by Thomas Hardy, Charles Baudelaire, and Elizabeth Barrett Browning, for example.

About three years later, in January 1931, Xu and his contemporaries published the *Crescent Moon Poetry Magazine*. Editor Xu positioned the magazine as the voice of poets, writers, and friends who shared several core beliefs. In particular, they believed that their new form of poetry had a brilliant future, that poetry was the distinct voice of their era, and that poetry was an art. Although the *Crescent Moon Poetry Magazine* lasted for only four issues, it served as a foundation upon which the group's new form of poetry could stand and take its place alongside traditionally structured writings. Attacked again by leftist writers, Xu and his fellow poets proclaimed that the spirit of love, as put forward in their poetry, could end the hatred associated with China's rising class struggle.

Xu notably avoided aligning himself and his group with any of the political factions gaining power, the decision to remain "apolitical," as Katherine Mansfield had recommended, was quite possibly a political stance in itself.

Sadly, Xu's lofty gestures toward spreading a message of altruism and positivity were not enough to cure his diseased marriage. With Weng Ruiwu and Xiaoman cavorting in the main rooms of their house, Xu retreated to one small chamber. During this time he penned sorrowful poems, including "Life," in which these lines appeared:

> You struggle in the bowels of the devil,
> Without a trace of light above your head.

Years later, Xu would write that this was a truly bleak period in his life and that, because of his broken spirit, he could only write about ten poems a year. When historians examine the reasons why Xu remained married to his second wife, they point out several possibilities. For one, despite her transgressions, he seemed genuinely in love with Xiaoman; nor was he willing to divorce her, which would have put her in a difficult situation socially and financially. For another, he most likely believed that he had to remain in the marriage to save face and maintain a noble image. He had, after all, made much of the profound importance of marrying for love. Yet when he did enter into a union based on passion, Xu found that his life had not only taken a negative turn, it had taken a disastrous one. In the decades to come, Xiaoman would admit that it was she who had derailed her husband's literary career, although she attributed this to her poor health, not to her drug addiction or her dalliances with Weng.

XU'S FINAL TRIP ABROAD: THE SEARCH FOR UTOPIA

In May 1928, Xu decided to break away from the complicated domestic arrangement at his Shanghai home. He left Xiaoman and Weng and traveled by himself back to Xiashi, where he celebrated his father's fifty-sixth birthday. His father sensed his son's depressed state and urged him to take another trip abroad, where he could escape from his domestic problems and possibly reignite his literary passions. With these objectives in mind and with the financial support of the progressive English philanthropist and Tagore confidante Leonard Elmhirst, Xu initiated plans to return to England and then travel on to India, where he hoped to visit Tagore. Xiaoman angrily voiced her opposition to this plan, but it was to no avail. Xu remained committed to his plans to venture abroad—a sign, perhaps, of his growing disillusionment with his marriage.

During this visit, Xu traveled to Germany and France, and then to England, where he met with Elmhirst at his estate in Totnes, Devon. The two had first met when the Englishman accompanied Tagore to China, acting as his business manager and secretary. Elmhirst was a wealthy agricultural economist whom Xu had come to admire because of his association with Tagore and for his visionary, idealistic beliefs. The philanthropist had established **Dartington Hall** in Devon, a utopian community in which members participated in arts and crafts, farming, and other cooperative activities. Xu visited him there in the summer of 1928 and wandered the property's large, impressive gardens. He later traveled to India to spend time with Tagore and visited Sriniketan in Surul, another utopian community that Elmhirst had helped the Indian poet develop.

Ever the idealist, Xu became captivated by the concept of the self-sustaining, optimistic, and forward-looking cooperative. He later wrote to Elmhirst about Dartington and Surul, calling the utopian communities a "heroic effort." He even sought the philanthropist's help to set up such a utopian society in China, a plan that in the end never quite moved forward.

While in India, Xu spent several weeks with Tagore in **Santiniketan**, a quiet town in Bengal, north of Kolkata. Here, Tagore had founded Visva Bharati, a school based on his ideals, where students could study in a natural environment amid beautifully designed buildings and gardens. Tagore had constructed several houses, including one stately multi-storied home that visibly reflected China and Japan's profound influence on him. Many of the rooms in this house feature polished dark wood and latticework that echoed Ming dynasty style.

The Indian poet and his young Chinese mentee likely spent their days together lounging on the low-slung Indian furniture in one of these handsome houses, discussing poetry, politics, and the fate of their respective countries. These weeks spent together established the pair as much more than star poet and translator; the two shared a bond that would resonate through time, beyond their respective deaths.

However, Xiaoman broke the spell of such idyllic Indian afternoons by beseeching her husband to return to Shanghai. In response to his wife's pleas, Xu boarded a China-bound ship in Kolkata and returned home in fall 1928. Though cut short, the journey to Europe and India enabled the poet to write "A Second Farewell to Cambridge," one of his most significant works. The poem is tinged with the melancholy he felt at leaving his beloved university. But it also echoes the joy he felt while wandering the English countryside and cobblestone streets of the place where he first embarked on realizing his literary passions.

CHAPTER ELEVEN

IN CHINA, FACING PERSONAL TURMOIL

1929–1931

TWO POIGNANT DEATHS

I
n late 1928 Xu received word that the health of his most influential mentor, Liang Qichao, was faltering. By early 1929 the older scholar was in critical condition. Despite the scathing critique Liang gave Xu and Xiaoman at their wedding, Xu remained extremely loyal to his elder. Leaving behind urgent work, Xu rushed to Beijing to be with Liang, who died on January 19 at age fifty-five.

Xu mourned his mentor's passing, but apparently he did not transform his grief into a work of writing, as might be expected. No poems or essays written by Xu exist to commemorate Liang's death—an odd omission given the fact that the young poet had written deeply thoughtful essays about his literary heroes Mansfield and Hardy just after their deaths. Strangely, he reportedly had not even read Liang's well-known book *The Collection of Yinbingshi* until he was on the train bound for Beijing for his last visit with Liang.

A few months after this sobering death, Xu received buoying news: Tagore planned to return to China. He invited the Indian poet to stay at his Shanghai abode, and during this time Tagore fans and Xu's students descended on the home to discuss and read poetry aloud in an impromptu literary salon. These

Xu in his early thirties.

vibrant fêtes helped the young poet shake off his depression, as well as Xiaoman's emotional hold over him. Tagore's visit enabled him to envision his house as a backdrop for more positive memories.

Xu continued teaching throughout the first months of 1930 at Kwang Hua University and National Central University, but he longed to be in Beijing, where most of his friends now lived. About the divide between his home base of Shanghai and his yearned-for city of Beijing, Xu told a friend: "Wonderful. All our friends are going to Peking. To go there, wings are all that a person has to have. . . . In Shanghai, you forever hide in your room like a snail in its shell." In October 1930 a riot broke out at Kwang Hua, prompting a mass cancellation of university classes and the resignation of a group of professors, many of whom then left the city. Watching his friends flee Shanghai, Xu lamented, "I shall soon have not even a single friend."

The solitude worked in the highly social poet's favor, inspiring him to write once again. On Christmas Day 1930, Xu completed his longest poem, "Love's Inspiration," in which this stanza appeared:

Thunder will make my voice tremble;
Suddenly spring and life will awake.
Inconceivable, oh, incomparable indeed
Is love's inspiration, love's power!

He wrote to a friend about his dissatisfaction with the epic work: "I am displaying my lack of talent in a long poem. . . . It is quite confused and disorderly."

Hu Shi was one of Xu's friends who had moved to Beijing, in this case to become dean of the Faculty of Letters at Peking University. He was deeply concerned about his younger friend's mental and emotional state, caused in part by a disintegrating home life, and decided to invite him to Beijing as a faculty member. Xu immediately resigned his Shanghai and Nanjing posts and relocated to the former capital. Although he tried to persuade Xiaoman to join him, she declined, instead remaining tethered to her opium bed and her paramour in Shanghai.

The spousal separation worked in Xu's favor at first. Having requested an upstairs room at the Beijing residence he now shared with Hu Shi, the poet settled into a far more peaceful and productive life. He thrived as a professor and had Hu Shi's library of favorite books at his disposal. As his solitary times at Cambridge and in Florence had shown, Xu thrived as an artist when he was alone and happy.

But this positive state was not to last. In April 1931 Xu received the devastating news that his mother had suddenly died at the age of fifty-seven. He quickly traveled back to his hometown, only to face more drama, namely that of not having a wife who could take on her filial duties. Traditionally, it was the responsibility of the woman of the family to prepare a deceased loved one for burial. But at that moment the only appropriate female in Xu's family was Xiaoman, who had no understanding of or interest in such practices. Thus, Xu and his father called Youyi to preside over the ceremonies. At first, she refused, claiming that a divorced woman should not interfere with the affairs of her former house. But Xu was in a desperate state. Youyi returned to the Xiashi family home to bury her former mother-in-law, taking great care to observe tradition. Following Chinese rituals, she placed a cloth pack in Mrs. Xu's mouth, dressed her in different layers of ceremonial clothing, placed her into her coffin, and summoned monks to the house to chant prayers for weeks.

Even though divorced, Xu and Youyi had become quite close friends, with Xu developing a deep respect and trust for his ex-wife. Youyi had not only survived the death of her second son, Peter, and educated herself to a high level, becoming fluent in German and English, but she had also thrived. Less than a decade after her divorce, she was a lauded businesswoman, having opened a popular Shanghai clothing store at which she often made bespoke shirts, pants, and ties for her ex-husband. Ultimately, she became the vice president of the Shanghai Women's Savings Bank and flourished financially, while her ex-husband languished. Indeed, she would sometimes hand the impoverished poet money so that he could pay his household bills, given that Xiaoman's opium addiction drained his earnings. Youyi always told Xu the money was from his father and never from herself, a way of allowing her former husband to save face. This relationship and Youyi's triumph as a successful, independent woman—only some two decades after the 1912 ban on female foot binding—reflect Youyi's fortitude and ability and the rapid progression of Chinese society during this era.

CARING FOR HUIYIN

With his mother buried and properly mourned, Xu returned to Beijing and attempted to settle into the quiet, peaceful routine he had established there. However, more sobering news came his way. Huiyin, Xu's first love, had fallen seriously ill. She was now living in Mukden, in the northeast province of

Liaoning, where her husband, Liang Sicheng, worked as a professor. Xu traveled there to visit his treasured friend. Assessing the poor state of her health, he encouraged Huiyin to return to Beijing for more advanced medical care and perhaps a better climate as well. In Beijing, Xu continued to watch over her until she showed signs of recovery.

Decades after Xu lovingly supported Huiyin through illness, she would ask Xu's former wife and their son Jikai, then twenty-nine, to visit her. It was a strange request given the two women's history; Xu had divorced Youyi because he had fallen in love with Huiyin in 1921. Nonetheless, Youyi agreed. Huiyin was "too weak to say anything, just looked at us and turned her head here and there," Youyi later told her biographer. "I think she asked to see me, though, because she loved Xu Zhimo and wanted to see his children. Even though she was married to Liang, she still loved Xu Zhimo."

Of the three women in his life, Youyi had done more for Xu than either of the other two—despite the emotional turmoil he had caused her. Decades later, Youyi's grown grandchildren asked her if she ever loved Xu Zhimo. They recall that she paused in silence for quite a while, then looked up at them and answered simply, "What is love?"

Examining Xu's personal life almost a century later, it remains clear that the poet drew from a deep well of emotion. The diehard romantic was simultaneously in love with Huiyin, married and devoted to Xiaoman, and divorced from but sincerely grateful to and admiring of his first wife, Youyi. "The whole of Zhimo is a mass of compassion and love," Hu Shi later wrote of his friend.

THE DESIRE FOR FLIGHT

Throughout his Beijing tenure, Xu had to struggle with Xiaoman's constant requests for him to return home. She wrote letters beseeching him to rejoin her in Shanghai. To avoid the fourteen-hour train ride from Beijing, Xu began to travel by airplane, which at the time was a highly risky form of transportation. One of his most famous essays, "Wanting to Fly," explored the feeling of soaring through the air and had attracted the attention of China National Aviation Corporation (CNAC), which wanted to feature Xu in an advertising campaign. In exchange, the airline had given the poet a book of free travel passes, and Xu used them liberally, even though flying CNAC was considered particularly dangerous; the airline was only a couple of years old, while the foreign airlines that serviced China had a longer safety record. Nevertheless, because of Xiaoman's continual pleas to her husband to return to Shanghai, Xu shrugged off any safety concerns and boarded flights with little fear. This lack of objective concern for his own well-being, coupled with his desire to placate his wife, would prove to be his profound undoing.

Xu did not make visits home to Shanghai solely to please his wife; he also attended to his publishing enterprises. During one such trip in August 1931, Xu published his third book of poetry, *Fierce Tiger*, through the Shanghai-based Crescent Moon Bookstore, which he still partially owned. In September he once again boarded an airplane and returned to his teaching post in Beijing.

At that point in his life, Xu was one of the most famous writers living in China, but even this renown could not save him from the fate that lay waiting for him.

In November 1931 Xu returned from Beijing to Shanghai, once again at Xiaoman's behest. There, he found not love, but chaos: Xiaoman with her opium pipe and her lover Weng. Unable to bear the domestic turmoil, he went to visit Youyi at her clothing store and told her of his flight plans. Hearing that he was traveling on CNAC, she asked him to consider flying on a European carrier, Eurasia Aviation Corporation, instead. She even offered to pay for the ticket, but Xu declined. He was in a rush to return to Beijing and wanted to board CNAC's flight the next day.

Xu had planned to travel to the northern city primarily to attend an architecture lecture that Huiyin was giving. She was still married to Liang, but the friendship between Xu and Huiyin had never diminished, nor had his affection for her. This much is clear from a Chinese Valentine's Day poem, "You Are Going," which Xu had written to her on August 20, 1931, and which concluded with these lines:

> The flowing luster of the stars will surge in the sea of clouds;
> Furthermore, always to shine through my heart
> There is the lustrous pearl that never grows dim.

Xu had originally planned to board a flight on November 20 but ended his Shanghai sojourn early due to domestic problems. A few days earlier, he and Xiaoman had had a ferocious quarrel—he had once again asked her to quit smoking opium, and she refused. Xiaoman screamed at Xu as he got dressed and walked out. In response, she threw her opium pipe out the second-story window, hitting her husband on the head. Unfazed, he continued walking. It would be the last time the couple would ever see each other.

CHAPTER TWELVE

A FIERY END

1931

XU'S TRAGIC DEATH IN THE SHADOW
OF A SACRED MOUNTAIN

On November 19, 1931, a day earlier than originally planned, Xu boarded a CNAC flight to Beijing. The plane he rode in was a small, 350-horsepower, mail-carrier plane. It traveled only ninety miles an hour, and he was the only passenger, accompanying two pilots. The plane departed at 8 a.m., with a first stop in Xuzhou. While on the ground there, Xu wrote a note to Xiaoman saying that the flight had left him feeling unwell and that he did not want to continue. Still, he was back on the flight when it ascended for Beijing—a decision that would seal his destiny.

As Xu's plane approached the small town of Dang Jiazhuang, in Shandong Province, a thick fog encased the vessel, effectively blinding the pilots. The aircraft crashed into the foothills near Mount Tai, spiraled to the bottom of the foothills, and exploded into flames. The two crew members and Xu were killed instantly.

An artist's rendering of a CNAC Stinson Detroiter
airplane, similar to the postal aircraft in which Xu
perished in 1931, in the shadow of Mount Tai. The poet's
plane crashed in the foothills of the region depicted here.

The beloved poet's death at thirty-five was a loss that reverberated throughout the cultural and intellectual circles of Beijing and Shanghai and left the nation's literati mourning.

—⟨∿⟩—

In "Wanting to Fly," published a year before his death, Xu had written a fantasy of soaring through the air. At the end of his essay he wrote:

> Suddenly the wings are slanting, and a ball of light swoops all the way down, clashing in a boom—and breaking up my imaginings while in flight.

A prescient vision, perhaps.

Mount Tai was the same sacred mountain that had captured the imagination of Goldsworthy Lowes Dickinson, Xu's Cambridge mentor. Dickinson had visited the mountain in 1912, climbed it for days, and marveled at the astonishing beauty of the famed natural monument. Indeed, the visit to Mount Tai and his understanding of the Chinese reverence for it left the Englishman convinced of the superiority of Chinese ideals. Mount Tai had also captivated Confucius, Chinese emperors, and millions of ordinary Chinese throughout the centuries—even Xu himself. In fact, the writer had immortalized the mountain in more than one poem.

In "Mount T'ai," Xu wrote that the natural monument "received in silence / The splendor of the sun, moon, and colorful clouds" and concealed stars "in the cores of rocks and beyond the towering sky."

It was in that same region, in the foothills near Mount Tai, where Xu's life would come to its untimely end, amidst the natural beauty that had so deeply inspired him. Hours after the accident, each of the three prominent women in Xu's life would react to his death in her own way. Xiaoman, most likely in an opium-induced haze, refused to believe the messenger who tried to deliver the news and sent him away. Huiyin heard the news the following day and was racked with grief. "The unbelievable and crude death," she later wrote in the essay "Mourning for Zhimo," "made the sky as dark as ink and blocked everyone's throat by sobs of grief." Ultimately, it was Youyi who accepted the telegram declaring Xu's death, and it was Youyi who broke the news to Xu's father and arranged for her eighth brother and her son Jikai to journey to the crash site and identify and recover the remains of Xu Zhimo.

BURYING THE POET

The education minister of the Shandong provincial government, a friend of Xu's, made funeral arrangements and notified Xu's family and friends of the poet's memorial service. Jikai and his uncle traveled to Jinan to place Xu's remains in a coffin. From there, the coffin was taken to Shanghai, where funeral services ensued. The family then held another ceremony in Xiashi, and Xu was buried at the foot of the compound's eastern hill. Hu Shi wrote the original epitaph, which read simply: "The Poet Xu Zhimo's Tomb." Some thirteen years after Xu's death, his father added a second stone. For this monument's inscription, a trusted female friend of Xu Zhimo, the author Ling Shuhua, adapted a phrase from the Chinese classical novel *Dream of the Red Chamber*. The inscription read: "The Cold Moon Illuminates the Poet's Soul."

An issue of the *Crescent Moon Monthly* was dedicated entirely to Xu's death, with words and poems written by his family, friends, and admirers. With an introduction by Xiaoman, Xu's fourth book of poetry, titled *Roaming in the Clouds,* was published in July 1932 and contained the poems that Xu had written during his final year.

In 1930, a year before his passing, Xu had written the poem "Love's Inspiration" and dedicated it to his great friend and fellow Crescent Moon Society member Hu Shi. Hu had helped Chinese literature progress from the traditional to the vernacular through his scholarly and popular work. Although Xu was not entirely pleased with this poem, the final lines capture a writer who sought the eternal through the beauty of nature and saw love as offering profound meaning to life:

> Now I can
> Really, really die, and I want you to hold me
> This way in your arms until I breathe my last,
> Until my eyes can no longer stay open,
> Until I fly, fly, fly toward outer space
> And disintegrate into sand, into light, into wind.
> Ah pain, but pain is of brief duration,
> It is temporary; happiness is eternal;
> Love is immortal.
> > I, I want to sleep. . . .

Xu's death came when he was at the peak of his talent, a fate that echoed the early deaths of two of his literary heroes, the romantic poets Shelley and Keats.

詩人徐志摩之墓

張宗祥題

中華民國三十五年仲冬

CHAPTER THIRTEEN

AFTERMATH

1931–1980

IN DEATH, NO EASY PEACE

Xu Zhimo sought excitement, intellectual engagement, and romantic passion throughout his life. Perhaps, then, it is not surprising that such a spirit would not immediately find peace in death. Neither his body nor his reputation were allowed an eternal rest, at least not for the first few decades after his death.

Although Xu was celebrated throughout his career as a poet, he and his body of work faced harsh criticism during various political movements in the decades that followed. During the Cultural Revolution (1966–76), for example, the political elite branded Xu as a member of the bourgeoisie and as a reactionary against the Communist forces that had started to gain power when he was alive. The Communists likely viewed Xu's literary concerns of love and passion as decadent; any work similar in tone was also attacked. Thus, Xu's books were banned, and many burned, along with the works of many other writers.

The poet's legacy was damaged in many other ways as well. In the late 1930s, during the second Sino-Japanese War, the Japanese had occupied his

Once smashed into two pieces by Red Guards, Xu's original tombstone was repaired and now sits in the center of a new burial ground designed by his distant cousin Chen Congzhou. The site is in Xiashi, Xu's hometown.

hometown, Xiashi. They set up an outpost and lookout point in Xiashi because it was strategically located on a major rail line, between two very important cities, Shanghai and Hangzhou. Ironically, it had been thanks partly to the lobbying of Xu's father, who had been a shareholder in the railroad company, that the railroad ran through their home city—thus making it an attractive location for the Japanese to control. In fact, the foreign occupiers went as far as using the poet's graceful family home as a military outpost. While stationed at the Xu house, a Japanese army journalist who wrote for a Japanese propaganda newspaper discovered two of Xu Zhimo's early diaries. These journals covered two periods in his life: 1911, when Xu was a teenager in high school in Hangzhou; and 1919, one of his pivotal years in America.

The journalist stole the diaries and took them back with him to Japan. There, he gave them to a friend who was a member of the Society of Chinese Literature in Japan. Soon afterward, World War II raged across the region, bringing destruction, death, and chaos to China, Japan, and the rest of Asia. Bitter animosity raged between China and Japan, and for about forty years, these journals essentially vanished from Chinese history.

The decimation of Xu's legacy did not end there. In the winter of 1966, thirty-five years after the poet's death, a crowd of more than twenty high school students traveled to Xu's grave, toting several 18-pound sledgehammers. Reportedly, they were young Red Guards looking to destroy vestiges of reactionary figures. The impassioned students swung their hammers at Xu's tombstone, a slab of dense stone that weighed about a ton.

Li Dejun, an old man who lived near the grave and watched over it, remembered arriving at the site the next morning to find a horrifying scene: Xu's gravestone had been broken in two and smashed. His coffin had been torn apart, and bones from his skeleton were scattered around the grounds, intertwined with rotting strips of his burial clothes. The poet's skull lay among the detritus.

The distraught Li had wanted to restore order to the destruction, but he dared not say anything or take action. During the Cultural Revolution, any kindness or sympathy offered to those seen as reactionaries could lead to profound trouble, such as being criticized and denounced in public. Soon the gravesite was stripped bare, even its once beautiful trees cut down. Eventually, a factory was built on top of the gravesite.

The ten-year period of the Cultural Revolution proved devastating to Xu Zhimo's legacy. In effect, his literature simply disappeared. For the two generations of Chinese whose lives spanned the era, it was as if the poet had never existed.

CHAPTER FOURTEEN

A POSTHUMOUS
RISE

1981–1991

RESTORING A POET'S REPUTATION

n November 1981 a high school teacher, Xu Yiyun, traveled to Xu's gravesite to pay his respects on the fiftieth anniversary of the poet's death. Xu Yiyun, a distant cousin of Xu Zhimo's, had been born in Xiashi, and as a child he used to play with his friends near where Xu Zhimo's tombstone stood. He remembered the poet's graveyard as "majestic." Positioned on the back side of Xiashi's eastern hill, the grave had covered an area of about sixty square meters and had a semicircular wall around it. A set of stone steps led up to a stone frame that held the poet's coffin. With the hillside's view of fields, stone bridges, cottages, and a winding river, the expanse of land felt "solemn and respectful."

After several decades spent living in another region, Xu Yiyun had returned to Xiashi to teach at the local middle school and heard that Xu's grave had been damaged. Still, he was unaware of severity of the site's destruction. When he got to the graveyard he found an empty area, deserted and abandoned, with the

This 1925 photograph of the poet at his home in Beijing was taken after he returned from his "sentimental journey" through Russia, Europe, and England.

broken stones scattered on the ground and wild grass swaying in the wind. Even the stone steps were gone. "I had already heard news of the grave being damaged in the Cultural Revolution, but I didn't expect that it had been destroyed so completely with nothing left," the teacher said. Xu Yiyun, who had read Xu Zhimo's poems as a child, surveyed the wreckage and choked back tears. It was during that visit that he decided he would like to convince the city to rebuild the poet's grave.

For days he searched the eastern hill near the grave in hopes of locating the tombstone, but he found nothing. He then went to an old teahouse at the foot of Dong Shan Mountain to speak to the peasant customers who lived nearby. After many conversations, he gradually learned that the stone materials from the grave had been taken away. Some had been carried off by labor camp workers who used them for their settlements. Neighboring villagers claimed other stones to create the bases for their cottages and pigpens. The local government had also appropriated many of the other materials to build bridges and roads. Within years, all the stones had disappeared from the site, stripped from the grave of a so-called reactionary writer who lived and worked during the heady days when China was a new republic, and put to use in myriad other ways to rebuild the now Communist country. Xu Yiyun said that this discovery of the grave's fate devastated him. "I felt disappointed and frustrated."

One day, Xu Yiyun learned of Li Dejun, the man who once took care of Xu Zhimo's grave. After many attempts, the teacher finally located Li, who had become elderly and crippled. Old Man Li, as he was affectionately known, could recognize the graveyard materials, made of relatively rare, dense golden stones, wherever they were used throughout the region. When asked about the poet's tombstone itself, the old man shook his head and said he had no idea. But Xu Yiyun could tell he was holding back.

The teacher understood Old Man Li's reaction. The region was still emerging from the ruin of the Cultural Revolution, and even though that intense political era had ended five years before, one still had to tread lightly. To show passion for a once-denounced poet could prove ruinous to all involved. Still, the teacher hoped for a resolution: the restoration of Xu Zhimo's gravesite and his honor.

Then one morning Old Man Li's great-granddaughter Li Minhua, a student at Xu Yiyun's school, approached the teacher to say that her elder had something to tell him. On December 9, 1981, Li took Xu Yiyun to a big village, Xi Qian Jia Dang, located by the Chang Shui River. On the southern end of the village sat a dock abutting the river. Old Man Li greeted the villagers, pointed to the top step of the dock, and said, "This is what you are looking for."

Xu Yiyun looked downward and saw a large slab of stone thickly covered with mud. One end of the stone was smooth, the other cracked. He asked a group of men working nearby for help, and with much heaving and grunting, they turned the stone over. "I stood there, praying from the bottom of my heart," the teacher said. When the men finally flipped the stone, Xu Yiyun read these characters: "The Grave of Poet Xu Zhimo."

As if spared by a higher force, Xu Zhimo's tombstone had been broken in two just beneath where the characters lay, and it only bore the scar of a big hammerhead on its top right corner. On the same day, Old Man Li led Xu Yiyun to another section of the river in the nearby village of Ding Gong Yan. Here he found the gravestone of the poet's father, Xu Shenru. It had reputedly been taken there to be smashed apart and repurposed as part of a bridge, but construction financing failed to materialize. The stone weighed about a ton, and it was completely undamaged, with all its original carved characters intact.

Xu Yiyun immediately wrote to **Chen Congzhou**, a professor and renowned architect based in Shanghai. Chen, who was a relative of Xu Zhimo by marriage, had written a much-lauded chronology of the poet. The gravestone discovery coincided with a new Chinese political initiative: "To clarify confusion and bring things back to order." Knowing that the poet's descendants had all settled and prospered in America and were connected to a large network of other overseas Chinese, the two educators concluded they could make a case to the government that restoring this once-illustrious poet's gravesite would foster relationships with the Xu family and other influential overseas Chinese. To this end, Xu Yiyun immediately wrote formal proposals to various government agencies and invited them to inspect the recovered gravestones in Ding Gong Yan.

Ten days later a group of authorities arrived in the village. The collective included Du Dexin, vice director of the County Cultural Bureau, Ma Yufang, vice premier of the United Front Work Department, and a museum curator from Shanghai. The men agreed that this was a remarkable recovery and that the tombs should be resurrected. The problem lay in a lack of funds for the construction and labor. Thus, the bureaucrats left Xu Yiyun in charge of guarding the stones until yet another miracle—this time, money—dropped from the sky.

Xu Yiyun had to coax the local villagers to look after the precious monuments. "I told them and Old Man Li that the stones were cultural relics of great importance, and that I was entrusting them to look after them," the teacher recalls. When they looked skeptical, he added, "I'm not asking you to do this for nothing. You'll get some rewards when we come to take them." After that speech, Xu Yiyun returned to the village every few days, bringing the villagers cigarettes and even snapping their photos near the tombstones. Today, the teacher still has those photos with a smiling Old Man Li and his cousin Li Defu proudly standing guard.

Now that the Cultural Revolution was waning, the unearthing of the tombstone of Xu Zhimo, who was once denounced as a reactionary writer, caused quite a sensation. Xu Yiyun wrote an article about the discovery that was published in *Economic Life*, *Xinhua News*, and China news agencies, and Hong Kong's *Da Gong Bao* published detailed reports of the discovery.

Chen wrote numerous letters lobbying for the government's assistance and finally received approval and funding to build the new gravesite. The highly respected architect was invited to survey the land for the right location. Since the Dong Shan area (the eastern hill) had become part of the industrial district, the group decided to move the grave to Xiashi's western hill. The project broke ground in 1982.

Chen Congzhou designed a new tomb and memorial site. The architect studied the plans for the original grave and then created a site that paid homage to the first but was scaled slightly smaller in size. He also built a tombstone for Xu Zhimo's son Peter, who had died as a toddler in Europe, next to the poet's (although Peter's remains are still in Germany). The grave of Xu's father was moved to the Shu Shan mountains. The new bottom halves of the gravestones were constructed of cement and hid much of the damage. "The crack of the old gravestone was hard to see, but the scar on the right hand corner remained there," wrote Xu Yiyun. "But it was unnecessary to mend—let it be a testimony to history."

In 1983, during the Qingming Festival (Tomb-Sweeping Day), Xu Yiyun, Chen Congzhou, and several government officials arranged for a mourning ceremony for the poet. With that, the grave was then officially opened to the public. Today, the rebuilt tomb attracts people from all parts of China and, indeed, the world. Elderly workers trim the hedges and bushes and plant flowers. In 1991, on the sixtieth anniversary of Xu Zhimo's death, a young fan came with a bucket of varnish to paint the characters on the gravestone. During the same year, a committee gathered to create and post direction signs for the road leading to the poet's grave. In essence, Xu Zhimo's grave and his reputation have been resurrected.

Meanwhile, the seemingly lost Xu Zhimo diaries would also find a happy end. In 1975, when relations between Japan and China had normalized, the Japanese presented photocopies of the diary to the Foreign Affairs Office of the Cultural Relic Administration Bureau, which then delivered them to the Museum of Chinese Revolutionary History. At that time, Xu Zhimo was still considered a capitalist reactionary scholar, and so the diaries could not be kept by the museum. Instead the original copies were sent to Xu Zhimo's son Xu Jikai, my father, who had resettled in New York.

By the mid-1980s, during the period in which Xu Zhimo's grave had been restored, the government sentiment toward the poet had changed markedly. Professor Chen Congzhou reviewed the journals and commented on their value. "Sorrow and pleasure overwhelmed me when I read the diaries," he later wrote in an article, "The Finding of Xu Zhimo's Early Diary Books." "It's been a miracle they still exist after all those years."

XU ZHIMO IN THE TWENTY-FIRST CENTURY

oday, Xu Zhimo's legacy has risen from the tumult of the Cultural Revolution to take its place in the literary canon of contemporary Chinese. His poetry is studied in high schools and universities throughout China and Taiwan. In 2000 a dramatized television miniseries titled *April Rhapsody* engaged millions of viewers across Asia. In 2013 *Xu Zhimo*, an ambitious CCTV documentary, was televised across Asia and on Chinese-language channels in the United States and Canada.

In the mid-1990s Xu's son Jikai gave the poet's Xiashi residence to the government to convert into a museum, which opened to the public in 1999. In 2012 the Xiashi government renovated and restored the Xu family home, introducing it into public use as the Xu Zhimo Residence Museum. Set in a lovely Shikumen-style two-story house, the residence recalls both Chinese architectural styles and Parisian design influences—the perfect homage to Xu's East-West legacy. In 2013 a Buddhist monastery in Changzhou unveiled a bronze statue of Xu Zhimo to commemorate his 1923 visit there and the poem "On Hearing the Chant of Intercession at the Temple of Heaven's Stillness at Ch'angchou," which he wrote about his sojourn.

Memorial stone at King's College, Cambridge University, commemorating Xu Zhimo and his famous poem "A Second Farewell to Cambridge." The stone was placed near the River Cam in 2008.

In the decades that followed the Cultural Revolution's end, Xu Zhimo's relationship to Chinese youth changed in remarkable ways as well. Whereas teenage Red Guards once desecrated the grave of the poet and his father in support of the Cultural Revolution's political dictates, today students journey to his gravesite on special occasions, such as the poet's birthday. At the tomb, they recite his poetry and sing pop songs, such as "A Chance Encounter," "A Second Farewell to Cambridge," and "I Know Not in Which Way the Wind Blows," with lyrics from some of his most popular poetry. They also leave offerings of flowers and writings.

In 2005 the Poetry Institute of China, Zhejiang Writers Association, and the Haining government began hosting the Xu Zhimo Poetry Festival in Haining every three years. In 2012 the event became an annual two-day event. The festival coincides with the anniversary of Xu's passing, November 19, and participants recite "A Second Farewell to Cambridge" each year in his honor.

In 2014 King's College at Cambridge University assembled an exhibition titled *Xu Zhimo, Cambridge and China*. It was the first exhibition about an Asian scholar to be displayed at King's College Chapel. King's College hosted the first Xu Zhimo Poetry Festival in Cambridge in 2015, inviting numerous scholars from China and Europe.

Halfway across the world, Xu Zhimo's memorial stone in Cambridge beckons to travelers and students from both the East and the West. The monument's luminous presence invites visitors to remember the Chinese poet who once sat on the edge of the River Cam, to explore his writings, and to consider the complex, ever-changing landscape he traversed in the early twentieth century as part of his expansive quest to forge a noble modern life.

XU ZHIMO, THE QUINTESSENTIAL MODERN POET

THE HEIGHT OF POETRY, THE ROUND EYEGLASSES, THE
AWAKENING
   AND LABORING ON EACH VERSE
A HAND REACHES OUT—IT IS LOVE, A POINT THAT IS SIMPLY
   IRREFUTABLE

KUIZE STONE, "XU ZHIMO" (2002)

Xu Zhimo is arguably the most famous poet in the history of modern Chinese poetry. He is not only known to academics and poetry readers, but also to the general public in the Chinese-speaking world. A national celebrity during his lifetime, Xu started writing poetry relatively late, after he decided to move from New York to London in 1920 at age twenty-three. It was his immersion in English literature and friendships with British men and women of letters that inspired his poetic exploration and shaped his literary taste and style.

From his letters, in which he mentioned reading the works of Virginia Woolf and James Joyce, we know that Xu was familiar with high modernism in the 1920s. Yet he was most drawn to romanticism as a result of both natural dispositions and aesthetic choices. He went on to become the most important romanticist in China. To this day, when Chinese readers think of romantic poetry, the first name that comes to mind is Xu Zhimo. Despite a short creative career that spanned from 1920 to 1931, he changed the course of modern Chinese poetry by introducing a new writing paradigm.

A punt moored on the River Cam, near
the King's Bridge.

Xu became interested in modern poetry in 1917 when Hu Shi, then an overseas student in the U.S., advocated literary reform of the stifling and decayed tradition of Chinese poetry. Instead of classical Chinese, Hu proposed a new poetry written in the modern vernacular—hence, modern poetry became known as "vernacular poetry." Instead of prescribed forms and prosodies of the past, Hu experimented with free verse and other forms borrowed from the West. Instead of stock images and familiar motifs in classical Chinese poetry, Hu advanced the notion of "poetic empiricism," basing poetry on personal experience rather than literary conventions. In the poem "Dream and Poetry" he famously said, "You cannot write my poems just as I cannot dream your dreams."

With the support of liberal intellectuals, especially those at Peking University, modern poetry flourished. However, it was also seriously flawed. The newfound freedom and the emphasis on accessibility often led to shallow outpourings or prosaic expressions. It was in reaction to this situation that Xu, along with his friends in the Crescent group, notably Wen Yiduo (1899-1946) and Zhu Xiang (1904-33), introduced a renewed sense of structure to modern poetry. In Xu's view, structure is essential to poetry; manifest in the stanzaic form and sound pattern, structure is inseparable from meaning.

An excellent example of this belief is one of Xu's best-known poems. Written in 1925, "A Chance Encounter" is a short poem of two stanzas with five lines each. The first stanza contains 9-9-5-5-9 syllables, and the second stanza, 10-10-5-5-10. Variation within regularity defines the form of the poem. The formal parallels echo the theme of ill-fated lovers: the twain is never to meet except for a brief moment—whether it is the reflection of a floating cloud in the water or the crossing of two ships in the night. The end rhymes enhance the affective quality of the poem.

Equally notable is the language. Unlike early modern poetry like that of Hu Shi's, "A Chance Encounter" is free of any traces of classical Chinese poetry, completely modern in its wording and cadence. When one reads the poem out loud, it sounds natural, fluid, and pleasing to the ear. Finally, the poem deals with the perennial theme of love, sad love in specific. Yet it is refreshingly different from most love poems in its nuanced feelings: instead of tempering down the poem's sense of wistfulness with apparent indifference or transcendence, the feeling is only made deeper. For all of these reasons, "A Chance Encounter" has been immensely popular among Chinese readers. It has also been set to music as a pop song.

In fact, to date seventeen of Xu Zhimo's poems have been made into songs. "Waiting for Cuckoo in Vain on a Moonlit Night" (1922), "In Search of a Bright

Star" (1923), "Sea Rhyme" (1925), "A Second Farewell to Cambridge" (1928), and "I Know Not in Which Way the Wind Blows" (1928) were also adapted into songs. "Sea Rhyme" was first adapted as a chorus by the famous linguist and amateur composer Zhao Yuanren (1892-1982), then rewritten as a pop song recorded by the superstar Teresa Teng (1953-1995) in 1974. The poem consists of five sections, each of which is addressed to a "Young Girl" in the second-person narrative. The girl lingers on the beach as the night falls. Rather than heed the narrator's warning about the rising tide, she refuses to go home and, instead, bursts into song and dances wildly. At the end of the poem, the girl disappears, supposedly swallowed up by the sea.

"Sea Rhyme" may be read as an allegory. The young girl whose singing and dancing cannot be repressed stands for the poet, while the sea that consumes the girl in the end symbolizes boundless freedom and imagination. As a Chinese romanticist, Xu espoused a poetics of multiple dimensions. He saw love as sacred and inviolable, he sang of the innocence of children and the beauty of nature, and he never tired of the pursuit of spiritual freedom. Along with many other poems from his mature period, "Sea Rhyme" embodies the pinnacle of Xu's accomplishments.

During the Sino-Japanese War (1937-1945) and the ensuing civil war in China between the Nationalists and the Communists, the writings of Xu were understandably eclipsed by the political turbulence. After the founding of the People's Republic of China in October 1949, he became a *persona non grata* whose work was unavailable to readers except as a target of criticism for its "petty-bourgeois" decadence.

On the other side of the Taiwan Strait, however, Xu quickly regained popularity for two reasons. First, under the Nationalist rule most writers of the May Fourth era were banned for either displaying leftist leanings or for staying on the mainland and for being, by definition, communists. Xu was one of the few mainland writers who were considered "safe" in postwar Taiwan. His poetry and prose inspired a new generation of writers there. In the 1950s to 1960s, Xu's poetry served as an important paradigm for many Taiwanese poets, who imitated his poetic form and structure, use of rhymes, and fluent language. Xu's lyrical prose, as represented by such pieces as "The Cambridge I Knew," "A Night in Florence," and "Self-Analysis," was widely read; the first piece even found its way into textbooks. His epistolary diary addressed to his second wife, Lu Xiaoman (1903-65), was extremely popular as well for its fierce individualism and intensity of feeling. The first entry begins with this sentence: "'Happiness is still not impossible,' this is my recent discovery." And the poet goes on to say: "I hate commonness, ordinariness, triviality, vulgarity. I love expressions of personality."

—ᘯᘯ—

The second reason for Xu's lasting legacy is the fact that his legendary life, as seen through the lens of his poetry and prose, mesmerized readers in Taiwan, while in China, Xu's literature was banned. His idealism, rebelliousness, and romanticism were endearing. His natural charisma and warm personality were remarkable. In his essay "On Xu Zhimo," the renowned writer and translator Liang Shiqiu (1904-77) recalls:

> It was Zhimo who was always gay and brought joy to everyone. Sometimes he was late, and the gathering was lackluster. The minute he showed up, it was like a whirlwind passing through or a torch lighting up every heart. He talked and laughed, gesticulated and moved about. At the very least he'd slap you on the shoulder or pat you on the face, he'd carry an interesting magazine under-arm or amusing letters in his pocket. He made everyone happy.

Another close friend, the preeminent scholar and pioneer of modern Chinese poetry, Hu Shi reminisced in "An Elegy on Xu Zhimo," written on December 3, 1931, only thirteen days after the plane crash that killed the poet:

> Friends could not do without him. He was our link, glue, and yeast. In the past seven or eight years, there have been quite a few con-troversies and disputes on the literary scene. Many who used to be close friends stopped talking to one another. But I have never seen anyone holding a grudge against Zhimo. Nobody could resist his empathy. Nobody could sever ties with him. He had infinite love, which brought people together. . . . He harbored no suspicions and no jealousy.

Besides charisma, Xu's love life was well-known to his contemporaries. If his unsuccessful courtship of Lin Huiyin is memorialized in his early poetry, his con-fessions of love to Lu Xiaoman became perhaps *the* model for love-struck young men and women in China and Taiwan. His divorce and remarriage scandalized not only the literary scene but the entire country. When Liang Qichao spoke at Xu's wedding to Lu, instead of offering congratulations, he scolded and warned the couple in front of all of the guests. It is also a widely accepted view that Xu's death was indirectly caused by the financial difficulty he found himself in as he tried to support Xiaoman's lavish lifestyle. Regardless of what one thinks of his personal life, by all standards Xu endeavored to live by his professed ideals. In poetry as in life, he was a firm believer in the divine power of love, for which he was willing to sacrifice everything, including life itself. His poem, "In Search of a Bright Star," presents just such a relentless quest. The protagonist in the poem rides a limping blind horse as he rushes resolutely into the night. At the end of the poem, the breaking of dawn witnesses both the horse and the rider lying dead in the wilderness from physical exhaustion. The poet who starts out as a pilgrim ends up a martyr.

Since the late 1970s when China re-opened its door to the West, Xu has not only made a comeback but become one of the most beloved and popular poets in the country. Beginning in the exhilarating new era of renaissance and "culture fever," scholars and general readers have rediscovered his long over-looked work and have been fascinated by his life story. Today, Xu is a household name in China, partly as the result of *April Rhapsody,* an extremely popular 1999 TV series based on his life.

Granted, there is a price to pay for such widespread popularity. Xu's poetry and prose tend to be treated as mere illustrations of his biography rather than being read for their intrinsic artistic merits. He is typically represented by a very small number of poems, such as "A Chance Encounter" and the beautiful opening and concluding lines of "A Second Farewell to Cambridge." Moreover, although we don't expect every reader to be a literary scholar, even these poems are understood rather superficially. This holds true even for some poets in China today who read Xu Zhimo's poetry without understanding its broader context and deeper subtext. To a large extent this misunderstanding led to the polemic on the poetry scene a few years ago when Xu was criticized for being "shallow" and romanticism was dismissed as a negative influence on modern Chinese poetry.

Such criticism is based on a misunderstanding of both romanticism and Xu. The dismissal of romanticism is underscored by an evolutionist view of literary history that romanticism is outdated and obsolete as a vibrant influence on contemporary poetry since it has been replaced by modernism and later trends. The criticism of Xu is most likely due to a limited understanding of his work and an antipathy to his immense popularity in contemporary China. As pointed out earlier, Xu's affinity with romanticism is based on natural dispositions and aesthetic choices. This affinity is comprehensive and profound. For both romanticism and Xu, the recurring themes of spiritual communion with nature, the power of redemption in the innocent child, eternity of love, and emphasis on creative imagination and freedom go far beyond a narrow sense of lyricism or expression of love.

In Xu Zhimo we find not only a very gifted poet, but also a new paradigm for the modern poet: iconoclastic, individualistic, and innovative. In Xu Zhimo we see a brilliant example of the maturation of modern Chinese poetry. In Xu Zhimo we reaffirm the confidence that modern poetry will have a bright future and take Chinese poetry to new heights.

Michelle Yeh
Distinguished Professor,
UC Davis, California

23.8.21

丝上的 露珠呢
　颗颗是透明的水晶球,
新归来的燕儿
　在帘幕里喃喃不休;
诗人们! 可不是春之女人问
　　送不闲放你
　　创造的"笑泉,
嗷嗷! 吐不尽南山北山
　　　　的璠瑜

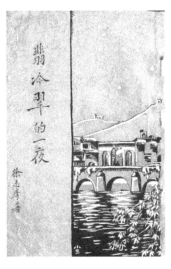

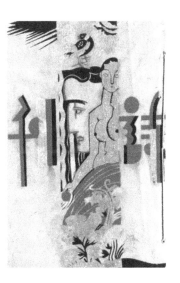

SELECTED
WORKS BY
XU ZHIMO

Original covers from Xu's
books and magazines for
which he wrote. Top row:
A Night in Florence, *Fierce
Tiger*, *Parisian Trifles*. Middle
row: *Shikan Poetry Monthly*,
Self-Analysis. Bottom row:
Zhimo's Poems, *Roaming in
the Clouds*.

Opposite: This first stanza
of "Dewdrops on the Grass,"
Xu's first formal poem (1921),
is hand-written by Xu and
includes his personal chop.

ON HEARING THE CHANT OF INTERCESSION AT THE TEMPLE OF HEAVEN'S STILLNESS AT CH'ANGCHOU

Like hearing, couched on one's back amid long-stemmed rioting grasses in the sunlight welcome as fire's warmth, the first summer call of the partridge which sounds from sky's edge up to the clouds and echoes from clouds back to the edge of sky;

like hearing, through the tropic air eiderdown-soft of a desert night when the moonlight's tender fingertips stroke lightly one by one the scorched fragments of rock, hauntingly, hauntingly borne from afar the sound of a camel bell which nears, nears, and again moves away . . . ;

like hearing, in a sequestered valley of the hills where the bold stars of dusk alone illumine a world bereft of sunlight and the grasses and the trees are bowed in silent prayer, an old fortuneteller, blind man led by a young boy, the clanging of whose gong reverberates through this realm of lowering dark;

like hearing, on some ocean rock savagely struck by breakers tiger-fierce while a black cloudwrack bandages tight the sky, the sea in low and gentle tones confessing its every crime before the storm's menace;

like hearing, among Himalayan peaks, echoing through innumerable ravines of shining snow the rush of clouds from beyond the sky driven by winds from beyond the sky;

like hearing, from behind the scenes in the theater of life, the on-stage symphony which blends laughter of vanity with screams of pain and despair, wild yell of rapine and massacre with shrill song of death wish and suicide;

I have heard the chant of intercession in the Temple of Heaven's Stillness!

Whence comes this godhead? Earth has no second realm such as this!

Sound of drum, sound of bell, sound of stone chime, sound of wood block, sound of the Buddha's name . . . as this music rolls and flows in stately measure through the great hall, stilled are the eddies of numberless conflicts, toned are the clashes of numberless bright tints, dissolved are the number-less hierarchies of men. . . .

This sound of Buddha's name, this sound of bell, sound of drum, sound of wood block, sound of stone chime (swelling in harmony filling the universe, loosing a speck of the dust of time) brings to fulfillment an endless number of *karma* centuries long;

whence comes this great harmony?—cessation of all movement, cessation of all disturbance in the radiant sea of the stars, in the pipe song of the Thousand Earths, in the flood of Destiny;

to the limits of Heaven and Earth, in among the hall's lacquered pillars, on the brow of the Buddha image, in the wide sleeves of my robe, in my ears and at my temples, in the pit of my stomach, in my heart, in my dream.
. . .

In my dream, this moment's revelation, blue sky, white water, warm soft maternal bosom of green grass, is this my birthplace, this the land of my belonging?

Shining of wings in infinity soaring!

Flow of joy from the source of Enlightenment, manifest now in this great, solemn calm, this calm of Release, harmonious, limitless calm!

O hymn Nirvana! Extol Nirvana!

Written in 1923
Translated by Cyril Birch

There are times when our little courtyard
    ripples with infinite tenderness:
Winsome wisteria, bosom bared,
    invites the caress of persimmon leaves,
From his hundred-foot height the sophora
    stoops in the breeze to embrace the wild apple,
The yellow dog by the fence watches over
    his little friend Amber, fast asleep,
The birds sign their latest mating songs,
    trilling on without cease—
There are times when our little courtyard
    ripples with infinite tenderness.

There are times when our little courtyard
    shades in the setting of a dream:
Across the green shadows the haze after rain
    weaves a sealed and silent darkness,
Facing my fading orchids, a single squatting frog
    listens out for the cry of a worm in the next garden.
A weary raincloud, still unspent,
    stretches above the sophora's top,
That circling flutter before the eaves—
    is it a bat or a dragonfly?
There are times when our little courtyard
    shades in the setting of a dream.

There are times when our little courtyard
    can only respond with a sigh:
A sigh for the times of storm,
    when countless red blossoms are pounded and pulped by the rain,
A sigh for the early autumn,
    when leaves still green fret free with regret from the branch,
A sigh for the still of night,
    when the moon has boarded her cloud-bark, over the west wall now,
And the wind carries a dirge for a passing,
    cold gusts from a distant lane—

There are times when our little courtyard
    can only respond with a sigh.

There are times when our little courtyard
    is inundated with joy:
In the dusk, after rain the garden
    is shaded, fragrant, and cool,
Old Pegleg, the toper, clutches his great jar,
    his bad leg pointing to the sky,
And drains his cup, a pint, a quart,
    till warmth of wine fills heart and cheeks,
A mythical Bacchus-figure,
    swept along on the bubbling of laughter—
There are times when our little courtyard
    is inundated with joy.

Written in 1924
Translated by Cyril Birch

IN SEARCH OF A BRIGHT STAR

I ride on a limping blind horse,
   Spurring it on into the dark night;
   Spurring it on into the dark night,
I ride on a limping blind horse.

I dash into this long dark night,
   Seeking a bright star;
   Seeking a bright star,
I dash into this vast darkness of the wild.

Exhausted, exhausted is my riding animal,
   Yet the star remains visible;
   Yet the star remains visible,
Exhausted, exhausted is the body on my saddle.

Now the sky reveals a crystallike radiance,
   An animal falls in the wild;
   A corpse lies in the dark night,
Now the sky reveals a crystallike radiance.

Written in November 1924
Translated by Julia C. Lin

JOY OF THE SNOWFLAKE

If I could be a single snowflake
Fluttering free in the currents of air
   My destination would still be clear
   Drifting, drifting, drifting—
Here on earth my place would be clear.

No forsaken lonely valley
No wooded hillside cold and still
   Nor to the empty alley's chill
   Drifting, drifting, drifting—
I'd have my destination still!

In my graceful airborne swirling
I'd spy the sweet place of her abode
   Wait till she walked in garden glade—
   Drifting, drifting, drifting—
Ah, hers the fragrance of plum-blossom shade!

At last in the liberty of my lightness
Gently I'd lodge in the bosom of her dress
   And seek, seek the soft surge of her breast—
   Melting, melting, melting—
Melt in the soft surge of her breast!

Written in December 1924
Translated by Cyril Birch

A NIGHT IN FLORENCE

You are really going tomorrow? Then I, I . . . well,
You don't have to bother, sooner or later there will be such a day.
If you wish to remember me, then remember,
Or else forget, while there's still time, that I ever
Existed in this world so you won't be sad in vain when you do recall.
Treat it as a dream, a fleeting hallucination;
Treat it as the withered blossoms we saw the day before yesterday
That trembled in the wind, shedding one petal,
Then another. On the ground they lay, trodden by someone into the dust . . .
Ai, trodden by someone into dust—into dust, that'd be at least clean-cut,
It's really torture to be neither living nor dead, to look
So shabby, unwanted, and to be the object of slighting glances—
Heavens! Why should you do it, why should you do it . . .
But I just cannot forget you. That day when you came,
It was like a ray of bright light in darkness.
You are my teacher, my love, and my savior.
You taught me what life is and what love is;
You brought me out of bewilderment back to my innocence;
Without you how could I ever know the sky is high and grass green?
Feel my heart, see how fast it beats this moment; and
Feel my cheeks, see how hot they burn; fortunately in the dark night
Nobody can see them. My love, I cannot even breathe now,
Kiss me no more, this life aflame I cannot bear.
My soul at this moment is a chunk of hot iron on an anvil,
Being struck by the hammer of love, again and again
Its sparks flying in all directions . . . I feel faint, please hold me,
My love, just let me die in your embrace with my eyes closed
In this quiet garden—how beautiful it would be!
The sound of the wind in the birch trees above, rustling,
Rings out a dirge for me; the breeze having come
From an olive grove, brings over the scent of pomegranate blossoms,
And takes away my soul. There are also the fireflies,
Sentimental fireflies who light up the way for me
As I halt my steps on the three-arched bridge
To listen to your grief-stricken calls; you hold in your arms my body
That's still warm, hugging it, kissing it, and tightly enfolding it . . .
With a smile I follow the breeze on my way again,
Letting it lead me to heaven, or hell, or anywhere,
So long as I leave this loathed human life to realize death

In love. Isn't this death in the embrace of love better
Than five hundred reincarnations? . . . Selfish? Yes, I know,
But I cannot bother now . . . Are you going to die with me?
What? If we are not together, the death cannot be "death in love."
To soar to heaven requires two pairs of wings beating in unison,
And even in heaven we need each other's care.
I cannot go without you, nor you without me; if it is to hell
That I descend, you would like it less for me to go alone.
You said that Hades is not more civilized than this world
(Though I don't believe it): a fragile flower like me
Surely will face the ravage of winds and rains, and then
Much as I may call you, you cannot hear—
Wouldn't that be plunging into a mire instead of gaining salvation,
Letting the unfeeling ghosts together with heartless human beings
Ridicule my fate, ridicule your timid carelessness?
This, too, has reason. Well, what shall I do then?
It's so hard to live, and yet unfree in death, not to say
I do not want you to sacrifice your future for my sake . . .
Ai, you said it's still better to live and wait, wait for that day!
Is there going to be that day?—So long as you live, my faith remains;
But you have to go at daybreak, can you really bear
To leave me behind? I cannot detain you, this is fate.
Only we know that when a flower is without sunshine or dew,
Its petals will turn yellow and dry so pitifully!
You cannot forget me, my love, only in your heart can I
Find my life, yes, I'll listen to you, and I'll wait,
Even if it is for the iron tree to bloom, still I'll wait;
My love, you are a star above me shining forever.
If perchance I die I will change myself into a firefly
Hovering low in this garden, near the grass,
From dusk till midnight, and from midnight till dawn.
My only hope is that no cloud will come over the sky
So I may gaze at the sky, at that unchanging star—at you.
My only wish is that you shine more brightly for me through the night
And across the sky to link the hearts of love together . . .

Written in June 1925
Translated by Hsu Kai-Yu

I

"Maiden, solitary maiden:
  Why do you linger here
  On the dusk-darkened shore?
Maiden, maiden, turn back!"
  "Ah no, I do not please,
  For love of the evening breeze."—
On the sand of the shore, against sunset clouds
A girl with wind-tossed hair
  Wanders at ease.

II

"Maiden with streaming hair:
  Why do you roam at will
  Here by the ocean chill?
Maiden, maiden, turn back!"
  "Ah no, first hear me sing,
  Sea wave accompanying."—
In the light of the stars, the cool wind carries
The high clear voice of a girl
  Rising, falling.

III

"Maiden, maiden so daring:
  A black curtain rips at edge of sky
  Storm tides threaten, rearing high—
Maiden, maiden, turn back!"
  "Ah no, see me dance free as air,
  As gulls in the spray disappear."—
In the fall of night, on sand of shore
Tenuously a shadow whirls
  Forsaken there.

IV

"Hear now the raging ocean's roar,
  Maiden, maiden, turn back!
  See the waves spring like beasts at the shore,
Maiden, maiden, turn back!"
  "Ah no, the waves turn not for me,
  I love the haul and plunge of the sea!"
In the chant of the tide, in the glow of wave
Through spume and spray in panic she turns
  Stumblingly.

V

"Maiden, where are you, maiden?
  Where now your song's pellucid trace,
  Your dancing limbs of slender grace,
Where are you, maiden so daring?"
Black night swallows the starglow,
  At sea's edge all light is hidden,
Tides abolish shore,
  On shore, no sign of maiden—
  No sign of maiden.

Written in 1925
Translated by Cyril Birch

What exactly is this thing called love?
When it came I had not yet been born.
The sun shone for me for over twenty years,
I was only a child, knowing no sorrow at all.
Suddenly came the day—I loved and hated that day—
When in my heart something stirred; something was missing,
And that was the first time I felt this pain.
Some said it was a wound—now, you feel my chest—
When it came I had not yet been born,
What exactly is this thing called love?

From that time on I changed, a wild horse without a rein,
Galloping over the wilderness of humanity. I was
Like the Ch'u man of old who tried to offer his jade,
Who pointed at his heart and said, "There's truth there, there is!
Cut me open here, if you don't believe me, and see
If it isn't a jade, this thing dripping blood."
Blood! That merciless cutting, and my soul!
Who is he that forces me to ask this final question?

What a question! This time I'm glad my dream is over.
God, I'm not ill, no longer shall I groan before you.
No longer shall I long for the ethereal; I've no share in paradise;
I only want the earth, and to live plainly and honestly.
Never again shall I ask what exactly is this thing called love;
Since when it came I had not yet been born.

Written in 1925
Translated by Hsu Kai-Yu

I HAVE ONE LOVE

I have one love—
I love the bright stars in the skies,
I love their radiance;
   There is no such divine light in the world.

On a cold late winter evening,
On a lonely gray early morning,
On the oceans, on a mountaintop after the storm—
   There is always one star, a myriad of stars!

Friends of grass and flowers by the hill stream,
Joy of small children on a high tower,
Lamp and compass of travelers,
   The eternal spirit shines miles, miles away!

I have a shattered soul,
Like a heap of shattered crystal,
Scattered among withered grasses of the wild—
   Drinking every sip of your busy sparkle.

Life's icy coldness and tender warmth
I have tasted, I have endured;
The autumn crickets cry under the steps; at times
   Have caused my heart to ache, forced my tears to fall.

I lay bare my naked heart,
To offer my love to a skyful of stars;
Let life be illusory or real,
Let earth exist or be destroyed.
   There are always the bright stars in the infinite void.

Written in 1925
Translated by Julia C. Lin

FOLLOW ME

The world is afraid,
Intolerant of love, intolerant of love!
Loosen your hair,
Bare your feet,
Follow me, my love!
Abandon this world,
Let us die for our love.
Let me hold your hand,
Follow me!

Let thorns pierce through our feet,
Let hailstorms break open our heads,
Follow me!
Let me hold your hand!
Come, let us escape into freedom!

Follow me, my love:
The world has dropped behind,
Look, the white sea,
The boundless wild sea
Leading into freedom.
Let us make love in this freedom!

Look where my hand is pointing!
There is a blue sky, a blue star,
There is an island with green grasses,
There are flowers, beasts, beautiful birds:
Come, take the small ship,
Sail to Eden,
Love, happiness and freedom.
Come, let us leave the world behind!

Written in 1925
Translated by Yuan K'o-chia

Again waking me up from a dream, a tune of p'i-pa in the still of the night!
    Whose sorrowful thought,
    And whose fingers,
Like a gust of chilly wind, a spell of depressing rain, and a shower of falling petals,
    So late at night,
    In so drowsy a world,
Are strumming the taut chords to send forth these disturbing notes
    To blend into the night in the deserted street,
    While a waning moon hangs on top of a willow tree?
Ah, the sliver of a moon, a shattered hope, and he, he . . .
    Wearing a tattered cap,
    With clanking chains on his back,
Laughs and dances on the path of time like a mad soul.
    That's all, he says, blow out your lamp,
    She is waiting for you beyond her grave,
Waiting for you to kiss her, to kiss her again, and again.

Written in 1926
Translated by Hsu Kai-Yu

A SECOND FAREWELL TO CAMBRIDGE

Quietly I am leaving
Just as quietly I came;
Quietly I wave a farewell
To the western sky aflame.

The golden willow on the riverbank,
A bride in the setting sun;
Her colorful reflection
Ripples through my heart.

The green plants on the river bed,
So lush and gracefully swaying
In the gentle current of the Cam
I'd be happy to remain a waterweed.

The pool under an elm's shade
Is not a creek, but a rainbow in the sky
Crushed among the floating green,
Settling into a colorful dream.

In search of a dream? You pole in a tiny boat
Toward where the green is even more green
To collect a load of stars, as songs
Rise in the gleaming stellar light.

But tonight my voice fails me;
Silence is the best tune of farewell;
Even crickets are still for me,
And still is Cambridge tonight.

Silently I am going
As silently I came;
I shake my sleeves,
Not to bring away a patch of cloud.

Written in November 1928
Translated by Hsu Kai-Yu

I KNOW NOT IN WHICH WAY THE WIND BLOWS

I know not
In which way the wind blows—
I am dreaming,
Whirling in the wavelets in my dreams.

I know not
In which way the wind blows—
I am dreaming,
Her tenderness, my ecstasy.

I know not
In which way the wind blows—
I am dreaming,
Sweet is the luster of my dream.

I know not
In which way the wind blows—
I am dreaming,
Her heartlessness, my griefs.

I know not
In which way the wind blows—
I am dreaming,
My heart breaks in the sorrow of my dream.

I know not
In which way the wind blows—
I am dreaming,
Dull is the luster of my dream.

Written in March 1928
Translated by Shau Wing Chan

Hardy, world-weary, life-weary,
　　This time has no need to complain.
Has a black shadow covered his eyes?
　　Gone, he will show his face no more.

Eighty years are not easy to live.
　　That old man, he had a hard time.
With heavy thoughts burdening him,
　　He could not let go morning or night.

Why did he leave sweets untasted
　　And comfortable couches unused?
Why did he have to choose a gloomy tune to sing
　　And the spices that burned his tongue?

He was born a stiff old man
　　Who loved to glare at folks.
Whoever he looked at got bad luck—
　　No use begging mercy from him.

He loved to take the world apart;
　　Even a rose would be ruined.
He did not have a gentle touch of a canary,
　　Only the queerness of a night owl.

Strange, all he fought for was
　　A little freedom of the soul.
He didn't mean to quarrel with anyone;
　　To see truth was to see it clearly.

But he was not without love—
　　He loved sincerity and compassion.
They say life is a dream;
　　Still, it shouldn't be without comfort.

These days you blame him for his regret,
    Blame him for his thorny words.
He said optimism was the face of a corpse
    Made up with powder and rouge.

This is not to give up hope;
    The universe will go on.
But if there is hope for the future,
    Thoughts cannot be taken lightly.

To uphold the dignity of thought,
    The poet dared not relax.
He lifted ideals high, his eyes wide open,
    As he picked at life's mistakes.

Now he's gone, he can no longer speak.
    (Listen to the quietness in the wild.)
Forget him if you will.
    (Heaven mourns the demise of a sage.)

Written in February 1928
Translated by Michelle Yeh

Last night,
And the night before as well,
In the frenzied madness of thunder and rain
Spring
Was born in the corpse of winter.

Don't you feel the yielding softness underfoot,
The caressing warmth on your forehead?
Greenness floats on the branches,
Water in the pool ripples into tangled longing;
On your body and mine
And within our bosoms is a strange throbbing;

Peach flowers are already in bloom on your face.
And I more keenly relish
Your seductive charm, drinking in
Your pearly laughter.
Do you not feel my arms
Anxiously seeking your waist,
My breath reflecting on your body,
Like myriads of fireflies thrusting themselves into the flame?

These and untold others,
All join the birds in their ecstatic soaring,
All join hands in praise of
The birth of spring.

Written in 1929
Translated by Julia C. Lin

ROAMING IN THE CLOUDS

That day you lightly roam among the clouds in the sky,
Carefree, delicately graceful, you have no thought to tarry
Along the sky's edge or the land's end.
You have found your joy in infinite wandering.
You are unaware that on this humble earth
There is a mountain stream. Your radiant beauty
In your passing has kindled his soul
And startled him to awakening. He held close to your lovely shadow.
But what he held was only unending sorrow,
For no beauty can be stayed in space and time.
He yearns for you, but you've flown across many mountain peaks
To cast your shadow in a yet vaster and wider sea.
He now pines for you, that one mountain stream,
Despairingly praying, praying for your return.

Written in July 1931
Translated By Julia C. Lin

ON THE BUS

There are all ages and all trades on this bus:
Bearded men, unweaned babies, teenage boys, merchants, and soldiers.
There are all the poses, too: leaning, lying down,
Eyes open or closed, or staring out the window at darkness.

The wheels grind out refrains on the steel tracks;
No stars in the sky, not a lamp along the road,
Only the dim lights on the bus reveal the passengers—
Faces young and old, all fatigued.

Suddenly, from the darkest corner comes
A singing, sweet and clear, like a mountain spring, a bird at dawn,
Or the sky lighting up over the vast desert,
Golden rays spreading to distant ravines.

She is a little child, her voice released in joy.
On this shadowed journey, at this dim hour,
Like a swollen mountain spring or a morning bird in ecstasy,
She sings until the bus is filled with wondrous melody.

One by one the passengers fall under its spell;
By and by their faces glow with delight.
Merchants, officers, the old and the young alike—
Even the sucking baby opens its eyes.

She sings and sings until the journey is brightened,
Until the fair moon and the stars come out from behind the clouds,
Until flowers on branches, like colored lanterns, vie in beauty,
And the slender grass rocks light-footed fireflies.

Written in April 1931
Translated by Michelle Yeh

On both banks of the river Cam are lush meadows which retain their verdure the four seasons round. Looking out from the upper story of the Fellows' Hall one may see in the fields across the river, morning or evening, always a dozen or so dun cows and white horses, hoof and fetlock lost in the rioting grasses, chewing away at their ease, while the buttercups that star the meadows sway in the breeze to the measure of their swishing tails. Each end of the bridge receives shade from weeping willows and oaks, and the water is clear to the bottom, not four feet in depth, and evenly set with long-stemmed water plants. These riverside meadows were another of my delights. In the early morning or towards evening I would often go to seat myself on this natural brocade, sometimes to read, sometimes to look at the water; sometimes to lie back and watch the clouds cross the sky, sometimes turning over to embrace the yielding earth.

But the romance of the river is not limited to the elegance of its banks. You must rent a boat for your pleasure. There is more than one kind: there is the usual double-sculled rowboat, and the light, swift canoe, and then, most charac-teristic of all, the long punt. This last is something seldom found elsewhere. It is about twenty feet in length and three feet broad, and you stand erect on the stern and propel it along with a great pole. This poling is an art. I am too clumsy a person, and from first to last was never able to master the technique. When you first start off to experiment, you are likely to swing the boat sideways across the stream, all ends up and stuck like a cork in a bunghole. The English are not a people given to open laughter, but be on guard for the eyebrow raised in silence! I cannot guess how many times the erstwhile orderly calm of the river was shat-tered by my novice blundering. From first to last I truly never learnt; and each time I trotted up indomitable to rent a punt for yet another attempt, one white bearded boatman would always comment with some sarcasm, "Heavy work, these punts, sir, and tiring on a hot day like this. Wouldn't you be better with a paddle in a nice canoe?" I would of course reject his advice, and with a touch of the long pole would move my punt out into the stream; but the result, inevitably, would be the truncation of the river one section after another.

To stand on the bridge and watch others punt, how effortless it seemed, and how graceful! Especially on a Sunday there would be a number of girl experts, all in white, their full skirts blowing gently in the breeze, each wearing on her head a wide-brimmed straw hat whose reflection trembled among the water plants. To observe the stance of one of these girls as she emerged from the

Painting of Xu Zhimo by Zhao Jiancheng.

arch of the bridge: the long pole resting in her fingers would seem to have no weight at all, yet when she lightly, casually touched it into the ripples and dipped ever so slightly at the knees, the punt would swing out from the shadow of the bridge and go gliding forward like a long green fish. The agile skill, the ease, the delicate grace of these girls truly are themes for song.

As summer begins and the sun's warmth gradually grows you rent a little boat and row out to the shade of the bridge to lie reading your book or dreaming your dreams, while the scent of the flowering chestnuts wafts across the water and the sound of the fishes' nibbling teases your ear. Or in a dusk of early autumn, to be close to the cold gleam of the new moon, you seek out a secluded spot far upstream. Fun-loving youngsters take their girl-friends along, decorate the sides of the boat with pair after pair of gay oriental paper lanterns, take a gramophone and pile soft cushions inside the boat. They, too, make for the lonely places to enjoy their outdoor pleasures—and who is there but would delight to hear that music borne up from the water below as it traces dreamscapes and bright hopes of spring across the quiet river!

For people who have grown used to city life it is not easy to recognize the changing seasons. When we see the leaves fall we know it is autumn, when we see them come green we know it is spring. When it gets cold, fill the stove, when it gets hot, let it out, change your cotton gown for a padded one, change your padded gown for a thin one: that is all there is to it. What is happening among the stars in the sky, what is happening in the soil underground, what is happening in the windy air, these things are no concern of ours. Let's get busy, one way and another there are so many things to be done, who has the patience to bother about the stars in their courses, the plants as they grow and wither, the transfigurations of the wind-blown clouds? And at the same time we complain of our way of life: in suffering, irritation, frustration, deadly boredom, who will claim it a joy to be alive? Who is there who does not, to some degree or another, heap curses on this life?

Yet an unsatisfactory life is mostly of our own choosing. I am one who has faith in life. I believe that life is not in the least as dismal as most of us, from our personal experience alone, tend to infer. The root of our ills is that we forget our origins. Man is the child of nature just as the petal or bird on the branch is the child of nature; but we, alas, are men of enlightenment, we enter daily deeper into society and remove ourselves daily further from nature. A plant that has left the soil, or a fish that has left the water—can it be happy? Can it survive? From nature we draw our life; from nature it is our lot to draw our continued suste-nance. What great, rustling tree is there whose tangled twisting roots do not penetrate down into endless depths of earth? We can never be independent. Happy the child who never must leave the maternal embrace; wholesome the man who stays ever close to nature. It does not mean that we have to go roaming with the deer and wild boar, or to seek out the caves of the immortals; for the treatment of the depression our lives present to us, we need only the mild prescription, "not to leave nature entirely ignored"—and there is hope that our symptoms will find relief. Roll in the green grass a time or two, go for a few dips in the sea, climb to a high place to watch a few dawns and sunsets and you will find the burden eased from your shoulders.

This is a most superficial doctrine, of course. But if I had not passed those days in Cambridge I could never have had this conviction. That spring—alone in all my life, though I grieve to say this—was not spent in vain. For that spring alone my life was natural, was truly joyful!—even though it so chanced that that was also the time when I experienced most deeply the agony of life. What I did have then was leisure, liberty, the chance to be absolutely alone. However strange it may sound, it seemed for the first time then that I distinguished the light of stars and moon, the green of grass, the scents of flowers, the energy of flowing water. Shall I ever be able to forget that search for the coming of spring? How many dawns did I brave the chill to walk alone in woods where hoarfrost covered the ground—to hear the speech of birds, to glimpse the rising sun, to seek the gradual resurrection of the flowers and grasses from the soil, to comprehend to the full the subtlest, most mysterious hints of spring. Ah, that's the cuckoo, just arrived, there on that dark branch to which a few withered leaves still cling, rehearsing his new set of calls! Ah, here's the first snowdrop thrusting through the half-frozen soil, and ah, isn't this a new wash of verdure over the silent willows?

Utterly still, this highroad gleaming with the damp of dawn, only the bell of a milkman's cart in the distance to touch in the surrounding silence with sound. Walk on along this road, and at the end of it turn off on a narrow path into the woods. Go on where the mists hang thicker, where the dawn filters palely through the interlaced shade of elms above your head; and still farther, right through the woods, until before you lie broad, level meadows and you can make out cottages, and the new green of wheat fields, and beyond these two or three low hills, dumpling-shaped, through which a road winds half-concealed. The sky's edge blurs in mist, and that sharp silhouette is the church of a nearby village. This region is the plain of the English Midlands, its topography a noiseless rise and fall like the swell of a calm sea; no mountains are in sight, only meadows constantly green and fertile farmlands. If you look back from that hillock there, you see Cambridge as nothing but a verdant swathe of woods close-set at one part and another with slender spires. Of the graceful Cam no trace is to be seen, but as your eye follows that brocade sash of trees you may imagine the course of its leisurely waters. Cottages and copses lie like checkers on this board; where there is a cottage there will be a patch of welcome shade, where there is a patch of shade there will be a cottage. This rising at dawn is the time to see the smoke from kitchen chimneys: as the dawn mists gradually rise and draw back the grey white curtain from the sky (best of all, after a light shower of rain), then the smoke from chimneys far and near, in threads, in strands, in coils, airily or sluggishly, thick grey or pale blue or white, gradually ascends through the tranquil dawn air and gradually disappears, as though dawn prayers of men were fading raggedly into the halls of Heaven. Only rarely is the rising sun visible on these days of early spring. But when it does break through, the early riser knows no greater delight. In an instant the color of the fields deepens, a gold powder like a film of gauze dusts the grass, the trees, the roads, the farms. In an instant the land all about is tenderly suffused with the opulence of morning. In an instant your own heart drinks in its portion of the glory of the dayspring. "Spring!" the victorious air seems to whisper by your ear. "Spring!" your joyful soul seems to echo back.

As you wait attendance on the river in her splendor, each day brings its own report of the progress of spring. Give heed to the moss-traces on the stones, give heed to flowers blooming among the dead grasses, give heed to variations in the water's flow, give heed to the sunshot clouds, give heed to the new-found voices of the birds. To the seeker of news of the spring the timid little snowdrop is a messenger boy. The bluebell and the sweet smelling grass are the first cries of happiness. The shrinking violet, the finely-etched iris, the fun-loving crocus, the resilient daisy—by this time the world is dazzled by the radiance of spring, there is no further need to bestir yourself in search of it.

Fresh brilliance of the spring: this is your time for roaming. Admirable transport authorities—here, unlike China, where does one fail to find a broad, level-faced highway? Walking is a joy, but an even greater joy is to ride a bicycle. Bicycling is a universal skill in Cambridge: women, small children, old men alike relish the pleasure of the two-wheeled dance. (In Cambridge they say there is no fear of the theft of a bicycle: no one cares to steal one, for the simple reason that everyone has his own.) Pick any direction you like, take any road you like, go along with the gentle grass-flavored breeze, let your wheels bear you far away, and I will guarantee you a tonic for the soul from your few hours' drifting. Pleasant shade and sweet grasses are what the road will offer you for your rest at any point you choose. If flowers are your delight, here at hand are meadows rich as brocade. If birds are your delight, here at hand are songsters of subtlest variety. If children are your delight, guileless youngsters are everywhere in this countryside. If friendship is your delight, here at hand are country folk who cast no suspicious eye on the stranger from afar, wherever you go you can "present yourself" like a wandering monk at the temple gate and find lodging for the night, with fresh milk and tasty new potatoes for supper and eye-appealing fruits for your delectation. If drinking is your delight, every inn in this countryside has laid in for your benefit a stock of the finest new brews, and if the dark ale is too strong, there is cider or ginger ale to slake your thirst and refresh you. To take along a book, walk three or four miles, select a peaceful spot, watch the sky, listen to the birds, read, and when you grow tired to lie back in the long tangles of grass and pursue your dreams—can you imagine a pastime more congenial, more the natural thing to do?

There is a couplet of Lu Fang Weng's,

"Send the call for a swift horse to greet the crescent moon,
Or mount a light carriage to take the cool air of dusk"

which describes the stylish pleasures of a district magistrate. Though in my time at Cambridge I had no horse to ride nor palanquin to carry me, I had nonetheless a style of my own: often as evening flamed in the west I would ride in pursuit, straight into the great flat disc of the sun at the sky's edge. There is no catching the sun, despite the boasts of Father Braggart, but by this means I was able to enjoy a good deal more than my fair share of the lingering beauty of the twilight. Two or three experiences linger to this day vividly as paintings in my mind. To speak only of sunset gazing: our only idea, usually, is to climb a mountain or to be by the coast, but in fact all that is needed is a wide expanse of horizon, and the sunset glow over a flat landscape can be equally wonderful. I sought once a place where, resting my arms on a farmer's fence at the edge of a great field of waving wheat, I could watch the transfigurations of the western sky. Another time, just as I came out on to a broad high road, a large flock of sheep came by on their way back from being let out to grass. The oversized sun struck their backs into a myriad strands of shining gold, yet the sky's blue was darkling; all that remained in the scarcely bearable brilliance was an open road, a flock of beasts. I felt a sudden mysterious weight press on my heart, and I actually knelt down before that trembling, fading golden glow. On yet another occasion, a sight even harder to forget: I stood by a meadow so broad that its farther edge was lost to view, where scarlet poppies bloomed everywhere upright in the green grass like a myriad golden lamps. The sun's rays, slanting from the edge of brown clouds, created by some magic a weird purple, transparent-seeming, a light hardly to be borne, and in an instant before my dazzled vision the meadow was transformed into—but better not say, for you would not believe it even if I told you!

It is two years and more, Cambridge, since I left you, yet who shall tell the hidden ache of my homesickness? If there is one thing of all others that I long for, it is to lie propped alone on the soft grass as the dusk, throbbing with the chimes of vespers, covers the spreading fields, and to watch the first great star shine out at the edge of the sky!

Written in 1926 by Xu Zhimo
Translated by Cyril Birch

A
CHRONOLOGY
of
XU ZHIMO'S
LIFE AND TIMES

1861

Rabindranath Tagore born in Kolkata, India.

1873

Liang Qichao born in Xinhui, Guangdong Province.

1842

The First Opium War (1839-1842) ends, resulting in key concessions to European trade demands. Britain seizes Hong Kong's New Territories.

1866

Sun Yat-sen, founding father of the Republic of China, born in Zhongshan, Guang-dong Province.

1881

Chiang Kai-shek, leader of the Chinese Nationalist Party or Kuomintang (KMT), born in Fenghua, Zhejiang.

1897

Xu Zhimo born January 15 to Xu Shenru, industrialist banker, and Qian Muying, eldest daughter of prominent scholars. Xu is their only child.

1891

Hu Shi, Chinese philosopher, diplomat, and writer, born in Jixi, Anhui Province.

1895

Thomas Hardy publishes *Jude the Obscure.*

1893

Mao Zedong born in Shaoshan, Hunan Province.

1898

H. G. Wells publishes *The War of the Worlds.*

1900

Xu privately tutored from ages 3 to 10. Proficient in classical Chinese by age 12.

Zhang Youyi born on December 29, in Jiading, a township of Shanghai.

1900

The Boxer Rebellion, a violent revolt against Christian missionaries and other foreigners in China, rages for 55 days.

1901

Goldsworthy Lowes Dickinson writes *Letters from John Chinaman and Other Essays* a decade before he travels to China.

1902

Liang Qichao publishes "On the Relationship Between Fiction and the Government of the People."

1903

Lu Xiaoman born in Shanghai in September. Raised in Changzhou, Jiangsu Province.

1904

Xu attends primary school in Xiashi, a township of Haining.

Lin Huiyin born to the first concubine of Lin Changmin.

1905

E. M. Forster writes his first novel, *Where Angels Fear to Tread*.

1905

The Chinese government abolishes the civil service examination.

1910

Xu attends the Prefectural Middle School in Hangzhou.

1910

The Bloomsbury Group, a collective of English writers, artists, and intellectuals, begins meeting. Foremost among them are Virginia Woolf, Vanessa Bell, Lytton Strachey, Clive Bell, John Maynard Keynes, Roger Fry, E. M. Forster, and Goldsworthy Lowes Dickinson.

Tagore publishes a collection of English-language poems called *Gitanjili* or *Song Offerings*.

1911

Katherine Mansfield publishes her first book, a collection of stories called *In a German Pension*.

Tagore writes *The Crescent Moon*.

1911

The Qing dynasty is overthrown by revolutionaries. Boy emperor Puyi abdicates and ends more than 2,000 years of imperial rule in China.

1912

Dickinson travels to China for the first time and visits Mount Tai, a sacred mountain in Shandong Province. He also visits Qufu, Confucius' birthplace.

1912

The Republic of China is founded and Sun Yat-sen is named the first provisional president in January.

The new republican government outlaws the custom of foot binding.

In March, Yuan Shikai becomes the second provisional president of the Republic of China.

1913

Zhang Jiaao, brother of Youyi, meets Xu while visiting the Prefectural Middle School. Zhang later suggests Xu to his parents as a marriage match for Youyi.

1913

Tagore receives the Nobel Prize in Literature, primarily for *Gitanjili*. He is the first non-European to win this prize.

1914

World War I begins (1914–1918). Yuan Shikai is president of the Republic of China, Woodrow Wilson is president of the United States, and Herbert Henry Asquith is prime minister of Britain.

1915

Xu graduates middle school at the top of his class.

Xu attends Shanghai Baptist College and Theological Seminary.

At age 18, Xu marries Youyi, 15, on October 29. They move into his family's Xiashi home.

1915

Virginia Woolf writes her first novel, *The Voyage Out*.

1915

The New Culture Movement begins (1915–1920).

1916

Xu takes preparatory law courses at Peiyang University (Tianjin University) in Northeast China.

1917

Xu studies political science and law at Peking University.

1918

Jikai, Xu's first son, is born.

Zhang Junmai, Youyi's brother, introduces Xu to the scholar Liang Qichao. Shortly after, Xu becomes Liang's protégé.

1917

Hu Shi publishes the essay "A Tentative Proposal for Literary Reform."

Xu travels to America for the first time to attend Clark College in Worcester, MA. While aboard the ship, he writes a patriotic letter home about China's future and his own.

1916

China declares war on Germany and joins Britain, France, Japan, and the U.S. in World War I. This move is made primarily to gain entrance into postwar negotiations.

The Warlord Era in China begins (1916–1928).

Chinese intellectuals, including Hu Shi and Lu Xun, promote the use of *baihua* or vernacular Chinese over Classical Chinese as a more accessible written standard.

1918

World War I ends on November 11 after an armistice with Germany is signed at Compiègne.

1919

Xu receives a bachelor of arts degree from Clark College with high honors in history and economics.

Xu pursues a master of arts in political science at Columbia University.

1919

Hu Shi publishes *An Outline of the History of Chinese Philosophy.*

1919

The Allied Powers meet at the Paris Peace Conference to set the terms for the defeated Central Powers. The Treaty of Versailles awards Japan control of Qingdao, formerly occupied by Germany.

The Treaty of Versailles sparks anti-imperialist student protests in China, and the May Fourth Movement erupts. The Chinese delegation in Paris refuses to sign the agreement.

1920

After completing a thesis titled "The Status of Women in China," Xu graduates from Columbia.

In October, Xu leaves New York for London with the hope of studying under Bertrand Russell.

Xu enrolls at the London School of Economics, where he studies under British political theorist Harold Laski. However, he leaves the program after six months.

Liang Qichao introduces Xu to Lin Changmin in London, where Lin serves as a representative of the Chinese League of Nations Union.

Xu meets and falls in love with Lin's 16-year-old daughter, Lin Huiyin.

Lin introduces Xu to Goldsworthy Lowes Dickinson, a fellow at King's College, who encourages Xu to apply to Cambridge University.

In October, Xu formally enrolls at King's College as an independent study student.

Youyi joins Xu at Cambridge, moving into his Sawston cottage. She becomes pregnant with their second child.

Xu separates from Youyi and moves closer to the Cambridge University campus.

Xu meets H. G. Wells and Bertrand Russell.

Lin Changmin and Huiyin leave England and return to China.

Bertrand Russell publishes *The Practice and Theory of Bolshevism*.

1921

Russell tours China for a year. The Japanese press erroneously reports that Russell has died. Xu writes a commemorative essay in his honor.

Following his return from China, Russell marries Dora Black, his second wife.

Xu writes his first poem, "The Dewdrops on the Grass."

Lu Xun publishes *The True Story of Ah Q.*

1921

Chen Duxiu and Li Dazhao found the Communist Party of China (CCP).

1922

A pregnant Youyi moves to Berlin to live with her brother. She learns German and gives birth to a second son named Peter (Desheng).

Xu is left alone with his thoughts after Huiyin and Youyi both depart from Cambridge. He realizes for the first time that he is destined to become a poet and writer.

Xu meets Youyi in Berlin to ask for a legal divorce. Theirs will be the first modern divorce in Chinese society.

1922

Katherine Mansfield pens *The Garden Party and Other Stories.*

1922

Xu meets privately with an ailing Katherine Mansfield in July. He later calls the experience his "twenty-minute eternal interview."

In October, Xu returns to China, in part to pursue Huiyin.

The Literary Society of Tsinghua University in Beijing invites Xu to lecture. His speech is titled "Art and Life" and delivered in English "in the Oxford manner."

1923

Xu joins Liang Qichao at Nankai University and teaches modern English literature.

Xu and Hu Shi organize a dining club that includes Beijing's cultural elite.

1923

In January, Katherine Mansfield dies of tuberculosis at age 34.

1923

The KMT and Communist Party of China create the First United Front, an alliance to combat warlordism in China.

1924

Xu teaches literature at Peking University.

Xu tours with Rabindranath Tagore and his entourage for seven weeks in China. As a result of his newfound friendship with Tagore, Xu rises to national fame.

In honor of Tagore's 63rd birthday, Xu, Huiyin, and friends stage the play *Chitra*. This event marks the unofficial founding of the Crescent Moon Society.

1924

Xu accompanies Tagore on a three-week lecture tour of Japan, where he meets industrialist Shibusawa Eiichi and the famous painter Yokoyama Taikan.

Huiyin and Liang Sicheng depart for America to study at the University of Pennsylvania.

Xu meets Lu Xiao-man and they become romantically involved, prompting threats from her husband, Wang Geng.

E. M. Forster writes *A Passage to India*.

Xu travels to Russia and Europe on a five-month "sentimental journey." He meets Thomas Hardy and visits Bertrand Russell and Dora Black in Penzance, England.

Peter dies at age 3 of peritonitis in Berlin, one week before Xu arrives for a visit.

Xu visits Exeter Cathedral in Devon, England, which inspires his poem "In Front of Exeter Cathedral."

Xiaoman writes to Xu, telling him that she is seriously ill. Xu also learns from Hu Shi that Wang Geng has agreed to grant Xiaoman a divorce. So Xu returns to China.

Sun Yat-sen dies of liver cancer in Beijing at age 58.

PERSONAL HISTORY

LITERARY HISTORY

GLOBAL HISTORY

1925

Xu becomes chief editor of *Morning Post Literary Supplement (Chenbao)* in Beijing.

Xu publishes his first book of poetry, *Poems of Zhimo*.

Virginia Woolf writes *Mrs. Dalloway*.

1926

Xu writes an essay titled "The Cambridge I Knew" about his fond memories of punting down the River Cam.

Youyi returns to China.

Youyi grants Xu permission to marry Xiaoman.

Xu and Xiaoman marry at Beihai Park in Beijing on October 3.

1926

Xu publishes a collection of essays titled *Fallen Leaves*.

1926

Chiang Kai-shek becomes commander in chief of the National Revolutionary Army and launches the Northern Expedition (1926–1928) military campaign against the warlords.

1927

Xu and his friends found the Crescent Moon Bookstore.

Xu and many members of the literati abandon Beijing for Shanghai as warlords and political factions endanger the city.

In the fall, Xu begins teaching at Kwang Hua University and Soochow University.

Huiyin and Liang Sicheng are engaged in America.

Xiaoman becomes involved with another man, actor Weng Ruiwu.

1927

Xu publishes his translation of stories by Katherine Mansfield and Voltaire's *Candide*.

Xu publishes his second book of poetry, *A Night in Florence*, and a book of essays titled *Parisian Trifles* in August.

1927

Chiang Kai-shek establishes Nanjing as the seat of the Nationalist Government.

In April the KMT carries out a violent purge, later called the White Terror, against Communists and dissidents in Shanghai. The anti-Communist campaign continues throughout the country for the next year, leaving more than 300,000 people displaced or missing.

Huiyin marries Liang Sicheng in Ottawa, Canada.

Xu travels for five months through America, Europe, and India.

Xu visits Leonard and Dorothy Elmhirst at Dartington Hall in Devon, England. He meets Irish novelist George Moore.

Xu spends several weeks with Tagore in Santiniketan, India.

Xu and Wen Yiduo publish the first issue of *Crescent Moon Monthly*.

Xu publishes a book of essays titled *Self-Analysis*.

1928

Youyi helps establish and manage Yun-chang clothing store, the name of which means "clouds and clothing."

1928

Wen Yiduo publishes the poetry collection *Dead Water*.

Xu and Xiaoman cowrite the play *Bian Kungang,* about a Chinese sculptor.

On November 6, Xu writes "A Second Farewell to Cambridge" on his return to China.

1929

Xu returns to China and accepts part-time English teaching posts at National Central University (Nanjing University) in Nanjing and Kwang Hua University in Shanghai.

Tagore visits China twice, both times staying with Xu and Xiaoman at their Shanghai residence.

1929

Liang Qichao dies in Beijing at age 55.

1930

Hu Shi invites Xu to teach at Peking University, which requires Xu to travel frequently between Nanjing, Shanghai, and Beijing.

1930

Xu publishes *Wheels*, a collection of short stories.

Xu writes the poem, "Love's Inspiration," which he dedicates to Hu Shi.

1930

New civil code gives women greater marriage and property rights in China.

1931

Xu's mother, Qian Muying, dies at age 57.

Xu and Xiaoman argue fiercely over her opium addiction.

While en route to Beijing on a fateful flight from Shanghai, Xu dies in a plane crash on November 19.

1931

In January, Xu publishes *Shikan Poetry Monthly* through the Crescent Moon Bookstore.

Xu publishes his third book of poetry, *Fierce Tiger.*

After Xu's unexpected death, the next issue of *Crescent Moon Monthly* is dedicated to the fallen poet and includes poems and essays written by family and friends.

1932

Roaming in the Clouds, a collection of poems Xu wrote during his final year, is published posthumously.

Goldsworthy Lowes Dickinson dies in England at age 69.

1931

Japan invades Manchuria following the Mukden Incident.

1932

The Japanese establish a puppet state in Manchuria called Manchukuo (1932–1945) and install Puyi as its nominal emperor.

1934

The CCP retreats to Yanan on the Long March.

1936

After Chiang Kai-shek is kidnapped by Marshal Zhang Xueliang in what becomes known as the Xi'an Incident, Zhang induces Chiang to end the conflict between the KMT and CCP and form the Second United Front against the Japanese invasion.

1937

The Marco Polo Bridge Incident marks the beginning of the Second Sino-Japanese War (1937–1945).

The Chinese attempt to stall Japan's rapid military advance in the Battle of Shanghai, the first major incident of the war and also one of the bloodiest.

Japanese troops capture the city of Nanjing (Nanking), massacring and raping thousands of civilians in the Rape of Nanking.

1937

Zhang Youyi becomes vice president of Shanghai Women's Savings Bank.

Xu's home in Xiashi is occupied by the Japanese army. Two of his diaries are carried off by a Japanese journalist and taken to Japan.

1939

Germany invades Poland, and World War II erupts (1939–1945).

1941

Japan bombs Pearl Harbor. The U.S. enters World War II.

1947

A seriously ill Huiyin asks Youyi and her son, Jikai, to visit her in a Beijing hospital.

1941

Tagore dies at age 80 in the Kolkata family mansion where he was born.

1945

The Germans submit to total and unconditional surrender on May 7.

The Japanese surrender on August 15 after the U.S. drops atomic bombs on Hiroshima and Nagasaki.

1946

Full-scale civil war breaks out between the KMT and CCP following the close of World War II.

1949

Architect and historian Chen Congzhou publishes his book *The Chronology of Xu Zhimo*.

1949

The Communists gain control of the country and found the People's Republic of China (PRC). The KMT are forced to retreat to Taiwan.

1950

Bertrand Russell receives the Nobel Prize in Literature for his writings in which "he champions humanitarian ideals and freedom of thought."

1950

The Korean War begins (1950–1953).

1953

Youyi marries Dr. Su Jizhi on July 27 in Tokyo.

1955

Huiyin dies at age 51 in Beijing.

1962

Hu Shi passes away in Taipei, Taiwan, where he served as president of Academica Sinica during the final years of his life.

1958

The Great Leap Forward, a movement instituted by Mao to collectivize agriculture, leads to grave food shortages and widespread famine. An estimated 20 to 30 million people die.

1965

Xiaoman dies at age 61 in Shanghai.

1966

The Cultural Revolution begins (1966–1976). The Red Guards, a paramilitary group made up of young people, exercise profound influence in China. Their mission is to destroy all vestiges of reactionary figures and old customs, habits, and ideas.

1966

Xu's books are banned throughout China by the Communist government.

1969

Youyi and Jikai help collect and organize Xu's papers for Liang Shiqiu and Jiang Fucong, the editors of *The Complete Works of Xu Zhimo*, the first major publication of Xu's collected writings.

1970

Bertrand Russell dies of influenza in London at age 97.

1972

Richard Nixon makes a historic visit to China. He is the first U.S. president to do so since the founding of the PRC. His meeting with Chairman Mao marks the end of 25 years of separation and opens up trade relations between the two countries.

1966

Red Guards destroy Xu's tombsite during the Cultural Revolution.

1973

Dr. Su Jizhi dies on December 20 in Hong Kong.

1975

As China-Japan relations normalize, a Japanese delegation to China brings photocopies of Xu's two missing diaries.

1975

Xu's poetry and literature gradually find their way back into high-school curriculums in China.

1976

Mao Zedong dies in Beijing at age 82. His death prompts the downfall of the Gang of Four, the group led by Madame Mao that maintained power over the CCP during the Cultural Revolution.

1978

Deng Xiaoping becomes the leader of the PRC (1978–1992) and enacts far-reaching economic reforms.

Reform and opening-up policies institute "Socialism with Chinese characteristics."

1979

The one-child policy is introduced in China to control population growth and alleviate social and economic problems.

1981

A local schoolteacher in Xiashi searches for Xu's tombstone and finally recovers it from a nearby river dock.

1983

Xu's biographer and lauded architect Chen Congzhou restores Xu's damaged tombstone and designs a new tombsite in Haining.

1989

Youyi dies at age 88 in New York.

1990

Popular interest in understanding Xu's life and poetry is revived during this period of reform.

1990

Deng Xiaoping's relaxation of political ideologies leads to increased economic reforms. Material incentives, such as increased income, motivate the work-force and drive progress.

1983

Arthur Miller directs a production of his play *Death of a Salesman* in Beijing.

The Commercial Press editor Zhao Jiabi publishes *The Collected Works of Xu Zhimo*, a compilation of the poet's writings, which Lu Xiaoman helped to edit before she died.

1993

Jiang Zemin is elected president of the PRC.

1997

Deng Xiaoping dies at age 92.

Sovereignty over Hong Kong Island, Kowloon, and the New Territories is transferred back to the PRC, marking the end of British rule in Hong Kong.

1989

The death of Hu Yaobang, a purged official, sparks pro-democracy demon-strations in Tianan-men Square and ends in violent suppression.

1999

After being abandoned and in disrepair for many years, Xu Zhimo's family home is declared a historic landmark in Haining. The Xu Zhimo Residence Museum opens to the public on September 24 during the Mid-Autumn festival.

2000

April Rhapsody, a TV miniseries about Xu's life, is televised across Asia.

2002

Hu Jintao succeeds Jiang Zemin as president of the PRC.

2005

The Poetry Institute of China, Zhejiang Writers Association, and the Haining government begin hosting the Xu Zhimo Poetry Festival in Haining every three years. In 2012 the event becomes an annual two-day event. The festival coincides with the anniversary of Xu's passsing, November 19, and participants recite "A Second Farewell to Cambridge" in his honor. The performance pictured below is from the 2015 festival.

2006

Jin Yong, a famous novelist and cousin of Xu's, visits the Xu family residence and calligraphs the epitaph that hangs above the entryway: "Poet Xu Zhimo's Old Residence."

2007

Jikai, the first son of Xu and Youyi, dies at age 89 in New York.

2008

A commemorative stone inscribed with four lines from Xu's poem "A Second Farewell to Cambridge" is installed at King's College along the Backs of the River Cam.

2008

The Summer Olympics are held in Beijing after many years of preparation. The event is a source of national pride for China and symbolizes the country's stature as an international powerhouse.

2012

After major renovations, the Haining government reopens the former residence of Xu Zhimo.

2013

CCTV produces *Cultural Documentary of Xu Zhimo*, a 20-episode film about the poet that is broadcast throughout China.

2014

An exhibit titled *Xu Zhimo, Cambridge and China* opens at King's College Chapel, displaying photographs and other objects from Xu's years at Cambridge University.

2015

King's College hosts the first Xu Zhimo Poetry Festival in Cambridge, inviting numerous scholars from China and Europe.

2012

Xi Jinping becomes president of the PRC.

2013

Lin Yin, mayor and secretary of the CCP's Haining Municipal Committee, visits Cambridge University to establish a cultural exchange program between Haining and Cambridge.

WEST（西）

術 語 表

東（EAST）

PEOPLE

ENGLAND

LEONARD KNIGHT ELMHIRST (1893-1974)

The son of a Yorkshire landowning family, Elmhirst studied history and theology at Trinity College, Cambridge University, and agriculture at Cornell University. He later became well known for his philanthropic endeavors. He married Dorothy Whitney Straight, an American heiress and the widow of a U.S. diplomat. In 1921 Elmhirst met Tagore in America and made several trips to India to work with the Indian Nobel Laureate. He also accompanied Tagore during his first tour of China in 1924. Leonard and Dorothy were interested in Tagore's work at Santiniketan, a utopian society and art college in Bengal, India. Eventually, Tagore's vision for Santiniketan deeply influenced Elmhirst and inspired him to establish Dartington Hall in Devon, England—an experimental rural reconstruction project that combined a focus on agriculture, education, and the arts.

CHINA

CHEN CONGZHOU (1918-2000)

Chen was the youngest of seven sons born in Hangzhou, Zhejiang Province. After his mother died early in his life, Chen was raised by his older brother's wife, an aunt of Xu Zhimo's. At age thirteen, Chen read Xu's essay "Wanting to Fly" in a school textbook and became enamored of the poet's writing. Chen was an accomplished artist from a young age and eventually studied under the acclaimed painter Zhang Daqian.

Chen devoted much of his life to preserving Xu Zhimo's legacy. In 1949, he wrote *The Chronology of Xu Zhimo*, one of the most important biographies of the poet. (The work also led to Chen's persecution during the Cultural Revolution.) Before she died, Xu's second wife, Lu Xiaoman, gave Chen a printed sample of *The Collected Works of Xu Zhimo*, which she edited, and manuscripts written by Xu. As the Cultural Revolution overtook the country, Chen had the presence of mind to donate the precious manuscripts to the Beijing Library and the Zhejiang Museum, thereby saving the work from destruction by Red Guards.

Chen rose to prominence as an architect of traditional Chinese gardens, and in 1980 he was invited to design the Astor Chinese Garden Court at the Metropolitan Museum of Art in New York City. In 1983 Chen, then an important member of the People's Republic of China Congress, succeeded in getting government approval for the reburial of the Xu family. Thus, he redesigned the Xu family memorial site in Xiashi, engraving the history of Xu's tomb on a rare golden quartzite stone and placing a copy of *The Chronology of Xu Zhimo* in the poet's mausoleum.

HU SHI (1891-1962)

Hu Shi was the son of a concubine and a government official who died while Hu was still a child. As a result of his father's early death, Hu received a piecemeal education from relatives and several of the new schools open in Shanghai at the time that taught English and other Western subjects. In 1910 he received a Boxer Indemnity Scholarship, which allowed him to travel to the United States to study at Cornell University. He originally enrolled in the college of agriculture but soon found himself drawn to philosophy. After completing his undergraduate studies, he went on to complete a PhD in philosophy at Columbia University, where he became a disciple of John Dewey. It was this intellectual foundation, coupled with his boyhood passion for popular fiction, that convinced him of the need to modernize the Chinese language. In a series of papers published in *New Youth* in 1917, Hu advocated the use of vernacular Chinese (*baihua*) in literature, a style that embraced the vocabulary of everyday speech over Classical Chinese (*wenyan*), which was difficult and required years of education to understand. He believed that the traditional Chinese language was China's greatest barrier to thriving in the modern world and is often credited as "the father of the literary renaissance" in China. A member of the Crescent

Moon Society, he became Xu's close friend and confidant. He was also one of the founders of the Crescent Moon Bookstore, which published many works by Xu. He was a major supporter of the *Crescent Moon Monthly*, one of the most important publications about poetry in modern China. After Xu's passing, Hu wrote the essay "Mourning for Zhimo," which reflects a deep understanding and empathy for his friend.

Among his many posts, Hu served as the Republic of China's ambassador to the United States and chancellor of Peking University. He ultimately fled China in 1948 after the Communists seized control of the country. From 1957 to 1962, Hu was the president of Academia Sinica, the foremost academic research institution in Taiwan. After his death, he was buried in a tomb close to Academia Sinica, which was later named Hu Shi Park.

LIN CHANGMIN (1876–1925)

Educated in China and Japan, Lin was a legal scholar and government official who dedicated his life to the development of constitutionalism in China. He was also deeply interested in poetry and literature and was a master of calligraphy. Lin helped found the Chinese League of Nations Union. He was close friends with Liang Qichao, whom he first met while serving in the cabinet of the warlord Duan Qirui. Lin became close friends with Xu during his stay in London, where Xu became enamored of his daughter, Lin Huiyin. In 1925, just as he had finished putting together a proposal for constitutional government, Lin found himself caught in a skirmish between warlords in Beijing and met an untimely death from a stray bullet.

LIN HUIYIN (1904–1955)

Lin Huiyin, the daughter of Lin Changmin, was a noted twentieth-century author and is considered China's first female architect. She grew up in a wealthy literary family and received an excellent education in both Western and Eastern subjects. As a teen, she accompanied her father to London, where she studied at St. Mary's College. Her months in London proved formative. It was in the British capital city that she first met Xu Zhimo. Additionally, Huiyin was significantly influenced by her family's English landlady, who was an architect. This friendship in part inspired Huiyin to study architecture, coursework she pursued at the University of Pennsylvania as part of her fine arts degree. Huiyin went on to study stage design at Yale University's School of Drama. In 1928, Huiyin married Liang

Sicheng, the son of Liang Qichao. In Liang, Huiyin found both a loving spouse and a lifelong collaborator. The couple, considered China's greatest experts on the history of architecture, devoted much of their lives to the preservation of Chinese architecture. Together, they visited thousands of ancient sites all over the country and wrote *History of Chinese Architecture*, an extensive study documenting the provenance of these Chinese structures. The pair was instrumental in founding Northeastern University's School of Architecture, where they both taught.

Huiyin contributed to the design of the national emblem of the People's Republic of China and the Monument to the People's Heroes located in Tiananmen Square. She was also a respected writer, poet, and member of the Crescent Moon Society.

Huiyin was Xu's first love, and though she and Xu never married, she remained a close friend and lifelong source of inspiration for the poet. For example, in one of Xu's most memorable poems, "A Second Farewell to Cambridge," he refers to a "bride," who is widely presumed to be Huiyin. Xu also inspired Huiyin's literary explorations. In 1931, shortly after Xu died, Huiyin wrote two memorial essays about him. She wrote another in 1935, four years later, when she happened to be passing through his hometown. Huiyin never fully recovered from a bout of tuberculosis she suffered early in life and died in 1955 at age fifty in a Beijing hospital.

LU XIAOMAN (1903-1965)

Born in Shanghai, Xiaoman was the only daughter of Lu Ding, a diplomat and scholar. Fluent in French and English, she was educated by French Catholic missionaries, and later by a British tutor. She also received training in the Chinese arts of painting, calligraphy, singing, acting, and Peking opera. As a young woman, Xiaoman was admired for her beauty and highly sought after. Her mother ultimately selected Wang Geng, a graduate of Princeton and West Point and a member of the Chinese Peace Delegation to the 1919 Paris Peace Conference, from her many suitors, and the two were married in 1920. Xu first met the glamorous opera aficionada in 1924, following his divorce from Zhang Youyi. Xu and Xiaoman's forbidden love was widely observed by the Chinese public, inciting sympathetic supporters and harsh critics alike. Once Xiaoman finally secured a divorce from Wang Geng, she and Xu married in 1926. This second marriage, however, spiraled into disaster when Xiaoman became involved with a fellow actor, Weng Ruiwu, who encouraged her budding addiction to opium. The turmoil caused Xu great distress, impacting his ability to write. After Xu's sudden death, Xiaoman devoted herself to collecting and publishing his work. She wrote an introduction to Xu's posthumously published fourth book of poetry, *Roaming in the Clouds*. Ultimately, Xiaoman overcame her addiction to opium and stayed in Shanghai after the founding of the People's Republic of China in 1949. Around that time, Shanghai's mayor Chen Yi gave her a position in the Shanghai Institute of Culture and History, and she supported herself by painting works for the Shanghai Academy of Chinese Painting. She died one year before the Cultural Revolution would seize the country.

ZHANG JUNMAI (1886-1969)

Zhang Youyi's second-oldest brother, Zhang Junmai, also known as Carsun Chang, was an influential statesman and philosopher. He was a pioneering theorist of human rights in China, establishing a small "Third Force" democratic party during the Nationalist era. He studied Confucian texts and left China for an academic stint at Japan's Waseda University, where he became interested in Liang Qichao's theory of constitutional monarchy. In 1918 he accompanied Liang to the Paris Peace Conference and went on to study philosophy at Berlin University, where he was influenced by the German philosophers Rudolf Eucken and Henri Bergson. He delivered a lecture at Qinghua University in 1923 titled "Philosophy of Life" that was subsequently published and sparked a national debate among intellectuals about science, free will, and the spiritual problems of human life. After the Sino-Japanese War, Junmai founded and chaired the Nationalist Socialist Party of China. In 1952 he moved to the United States, where he died in 1969.

ZHANG JIAAO (1889-1979)

Zhang Youyi's fourth-oldest brother, Zhang Jiaao, was a leading innovator in the history of China's modern banking system. Like his brother, Jiaao went to Japan to study finance and economics at Keio University. When he returned to China in 1909, he began his public service career in the Qing government's ministry of communications and edited its official gazette. In 1913 Jiaao was appointed assistant manager of the Bank of China's Shanghai branch. He rose to prominence in 1916 when he refused to follow orders from Yuan Shikai to suspend the redemption of notes. Though an order for his arrest was issued at the time, the public supported his decision and he was later promoted to general manager, a position he held for six years. Jiaao was instrumental in establishing a separation between government and banking institutions. In 1935 he became China's minister of railways (the ministry was merged with the ministry of communications during the Sino-Japanese War) and contributed greatly to the financing and construction of national railways. Jiaao eventually moved to America in 1953, becoming a senior research fellow at the Hoover Institution at Stanford University. He lived there until his death in 1979.

INFLUENTIAL GROUPS

BLOOMSBURY GROUP

The Bloomsburies, as they were also known, were a fluid group of English writers, artists, and philosophers, most of whom had ties to Cambridge University. They were both widely praised and criticized for many of their beliefs and work in art, literature, economics, and political and social theory. Predominantly reformist in nature, the group questioned and confronted many of the religious, artistic, social, and sexual attitudes of the time. The group was named after London's Bloomsbury district and existed primarily from 1904 to the late 1930s. The writers Virginia Woolf and E. M. Forster, the artist Vanessa Bell, the biographer Lytton Strachey, and the economist John Maynard Keynes were among its key members. Xu interacted socially with several group members and was deeply influenced by such friends and mentors as Bertrand Russell and Roger Fry.

CRESCENT MOON SOCIETY

This group of Chinese writers and intellectuals, many educated in England, took its name from a collection of poems by Tagore. The society was unofficially founded in 1924 on the night of Xu and Lin Huiyin's performance of the play *Chitra* for Tagore on his sixty-third birthday. Xu is considered one of the key founders of the group, which in many ways paralleled England's Bloomsbury Group. Other notable members included such cognoscenti as the philosopher Hu Shi, the poet Wen Yiduo, the writer Liang Shiqiu, the writer Shen Congwen, the architect and writer Lin Huiyin, and the artist and writer Ling Shuhua. As supporters of the New Culture Movement, group members espoused progressive beliefs, which ultimately led Communists and other leftists to attack them.

The society existed roughly from 1923 to 1931, disbanding shortly after Xu's sudden death.

EVENTS AND TERMS

FALL OF THE QING DYNASTY AND THE FOUNDING OF THE REPUBLIC OF CHINA (1911–1912)

By the mid-nineteenth century, Japan and many Western powers, such as England, France, and America, had begun occupying the treaty ports of Shanghai and Guangdong, among other cities in China. This situation both humbled and threatened China and prompted Chinese Nationalists to pressure the Qing government for change. Nationalists called for a less parochial system and more progressive and unifying ideas for running the country.

In response, the Qing court's Manchu government made efforts at constitutional reform. For example, it abolished the examination system, which had given power primarily to elites, modernized its military, and decentralized its power by creating elected assemblies and increasing provincial self-government.

Still, millions of Chinese began pressing for widespread reform or outright revolution. Kang Youwei and Liang Qichao led those who wanted a constitutional monarchy. Dr. Sun Yat-sen led a variety of groups that together formed the Revolutionary Alliance, a resistance movement that strove to replace Qing rule with a republican government.

Sun's Revolutionary Alliance orchestrated several different revolts against the Qing, but each revolt was quelled by the Qing army. Finally, on October 10, 1911, an uprising in Wuchang erupted into a grand-scale rebellion.

As a result of that revolt, Sun became the provisional president of the newly declared Republic of China, and the Qing royal family abdicated the throne on February 12, 1912. This ended over two thousand years of imperial rule and began the Republican Era in China.

CLASSICAL AND VERNACULAR CHINESE

Classical Chinese is primarily a literary language that is more formal and traditional than spoken, or vernacular, Chinese. As a result, most of the important works of Chinese scholarship and thought are written in Classical Chinese and require substantial education and training to understand.

Classical Chinese remained the standard literary form up until the early twentieth century, when such intellectuals as Hu Shi and Chen Duxiu began to challenge its efficacy in a modernizing China. In several essays published in *New Youth* in 1917, Hu Shi advocated for the use of a written vernacular Chinese that would more closely reflect modern Chinese as it is spoken. The transition to a written vernacular that utilizes the colloquial vocabulary of everyday people guaranteed accessibility and ultimately had the effect of opening up literature to a wider audience and making the dissemination of knowledge and new ideas much easier.

NEW CULTURE MOVEMENT

China's New Culture Movement (NCM) gained strength from about 1912 to 1919, approximately one decade before the Nationalists (the Kuomintang) came to power. Intellectuals founded the movement, which sprang from their disillusionment with traditional Chinese culture and the failure of the 1912 Chinese Republic to address China's widespread societal problems and political issues. Scholars such as Chen Duxiu, Cai Yuanpei, Li Dazhao, Lu Xun, and Hu Shi revolted against Confucian culture in their writings and public speeches. Their vision was to create a new Chinese culture based on global and Western standards; in particular, one that examined China's perspective on democracy and science.

For the country's progressive intellectuals, democracy was seen as a way to stabilize China's political fluctuations. Similarly, they viewed Western science as a tool to eradicate the "darkness of ignorance and superstition." During this era, scholars and women also supported a rising feminist movement as a way to combat traditional values and restructure the prevailing patriarchal family hierarchy.

NCM leaders also advocated for a new vernacular language and greater individual freedom. Activists pushed for a reexamination of Confucian texts and ancient classics using modern critical methods, the instillation of egalitarian values, and a stronger vision of China's future, as opposed to resting on its past accomplishments and power.

The ideas discussed throughout the NCM did not remain merely theoretical. In fact, national debates led to the momentous May Fourth Movement of 1919, when students in Beijing protested the Paris Peace Conference, at which Japan was awarded occupation rights to Shandong. The Paris Peace dispute then erupted into a nationwide anti-foreign movement, with student demonstrators rallying against imperialism and becoming increasingly nationalistic.

Student protestors also discovered the power of political mobilization, drawing from a populist base of demonstrators, rather than one based solely on intellectual elites. In addition, many movement leaders began publishing political writings in vernacular language—a way for a greater number of people, with varying levels of education, to read more easily the latest manifestos. Western doctrines became fashionable, especially those that supported cultural criticism and the idea of nation building.

BOXER INDEMNITY SCHOLARSHIP PROGRAM

Following the Boxer Rebellion (1898–1900), the defeated Qing dynasty was forced to pay about $333 million to the Eight Nation Alliance that had defeated it. The Chinese believed they had been forced to pay too much and demanded that some of it be returned. Although the overage was not remitted directly, in 1906 President Theodore Roosevelt was persuaded by Edmund James, the president of the University of Illinois, and Arthur Henderson Smith, an American missionary, to use it to establish the Boxer Indemnity Scholarship Program which would allow Chinese students to study in the United States. Hu Shi, Lin

Huiyin, and Liang Sicheng all benefited from support they received from this fund.

MAY FOURTH MOVEMENT

The May Fourth Movement, a national uprising in China led by intellectuals and students, stood as a defining event for many young, forward-looking Chinese. Helmed by scholars who introduced new cultural ideas like science, patriotism, and anti-imperialism to the masses, the movement exploded on May 4, 1919.

The uprising erupted in response to a momentous decision made at the Versailles Peace Conference on April 28, 1919: a treaty signed by the European powers gave Japan control of China's Shandong Province. Under the orders of Xu Shichang, president of the Beiyang government, Liang Qichao attended the conference in Versailles. Liang realized that the Beiyang government, under the control of the Chinese warlord and politician Duan Qirui, intended to accept Japanese rights to Shandong. Liang telegraphed Lin Changmin to convey the news and appealed to the Western Allies to return control over Shandong to the Chinese. Nevertheless, on April 29, 1919, the Western Allies awarded rights to Shandong to the Japanese.

In response, Lin Changmin published an essay in the *Morning Post* on May 2 urging the entire country to protect Shandong from falling into Japanese hands.

On May 4, the news from Versailles, coupled with Lin's published appeal, sparked an enormous protest by some three thousand students at thirteen Beijing universities. During the demonstrations, protestors declared that China would not accept the concession of Chinese territory to Japan and called for a nationwide boycott of Japanese goods. Students rioted, burned down buildings, and demanded the resignation of corrupt officials.

The May Fourth Movement marked a radical shift in Chinese thinking and behavior. It broke with traditional deference to authority and demonstrated the might of the average man. Intellectuals continued to write manifestos that called for social revolution, challenged traditional Confucian values and deference to authority, and encouraged self-expression.

WARLORDS

Warlords were independent military commanders who gained regional power in China from 1916 to 1928. Following the death of China's first president, Yuan

Shikai, the warlords ruled various areas of the country. Beiyang's warlords were the most powerful. China's ten major warlords had all served in the Beiying army under Yuan and achieved power by backing provincial military interests. Sometimes they were backed by foreign powers like Japan. No single warlord ever became powerful enough to destroy all of the rest. Thus, they were each able to control only one or two provinces.

During the 1920s, these factions fought for control of territory and government positions. Meanwhile, in the South, Sun Yat-sen had established an independent revolutionary regime under the control of the Nationalist Party, which received aid to build the republican army from the then-small Chinese Communist Party and the Soviet Union. With this army, the Nationalists were able to control the South.

Although Sun died in 1925, the Nationalist Party continued to grow in influence and power. In 1926 the Nationalist forces under Chiang Kai-shek swept northward, a military move that was called the Northern Expedition and captured warlord territories. By 1928 Chiang's forces were able to abolish many of the separate warlord regimes and reunify China.

Chiang did not eliminate the warlords but formed alliances and incorporated them into his army. Warlords continued to exert some power over their own domains and remained a force in Chinese politics until the establishment of the communist government in 1949.

PLACES

SANTINIKETAN

Santiniketan, which means "abode of peace" in Sanskrit, was first established as an ashram and spiritual center by Rabindranath Tagore's father, Debendranath Tagore, in 1888. The younger Tagore would later found several schools on the property over the course of several decades, ultimately culminating in his life's work of exploring the life of the mind in conjunction with a program of promoting practical education in the crafts and an appreciation for the natural world.

It wasn't until the 1890s, when Tagore was in his thirties, that he became estate manager of Santiniketan, located in the rural hinterlands of Bengal 158 kilometers northwest of Kolkata. There, his eyes were opened to the difficulties of village life. The experience humbled him and made him ashamed of his wealthy family's landlord status. He wanted to find a way to educate the villagers and help lift them from both mental and material poverty.

On December 22, 1901, he founded a school named Brahmacharya Ashram in the tradition of ancient forest hermitages. This school embraced the gurukul tradition of residential schooling where students learn from their guru or teacher in nature, with the open air and a canopy of trees for a classroom.

In 1921, on a trip to New York, Tagore invited Leonard Elmhirst, then a student of agricultural economics at Cornell University, to help him to found a new school to commence a project of rural reconstruction. At the end of that same year, Tagore formally founded the Visva Bharati school, which was given the status of university in 1951 and remains one of the top schools in India today.

The following year he opened Sriniketan, which means "abode of plenty," with Leonard as its first director and funding from the American heiress Dorothy Whitney Straight (who later married Leonard). They taught peasants self-reliance through practical crafts like alpona, batik, and leatherwork and, most importantly, how to increase agricultural production through the use of Western science. The four years Leonard spent in India running the school at Sriniketan, where he trained staff and worked with students to fix latrines, cultivate gardens, and build houses and workshops, proved instrumental to Tagore's legacy of rural reconstruction at Santiniketan.

Tagore's ultimate vision, which some have termed utopian, was to organize the villages so that they could become self-sufficient on a cooperative basis. Over two decades, Tagore's reconstruction work, which began in the rural village of Surul, spread to twenty-two villages.

Humanist that he was, Tagore invited visitors from all over the world to speak at Santiniketan in hopes of facilitating a greater understanding among cultures. His educational experiment deeply influenced future visionaries around the world, including his own countryman Mahatma Gandhi, who would later found similar ashrams at Wardha and Sewagram.

Similarly, Leonard's experiences and conversations with Tagore helped him shape plans for Dartington Hall, a utopian society he and Dorothy later established in Devon, England. Xu Zhimo, in turn, would be greatly inspired by Santiniketan and the activities under way at Dartington when he visited the Elmhirsts there in 1928.

DARTINGTON HALL

Leonard and Dorothy Whitney Elmhirst were social pioneers deeply interested in fostering progressive education and rural reconstruction in Britain. They founded Dartington Hall with the hope of creating a more collaborative, resilient, and creative society.

Elmhirst, who helped Rabindranath Tagore establish Sriniketan in 1922 and served as its director for four years, was deeply affected by the time he spent in India working with students and the local villagers. He also served as the Indian poet's secretary and accompanied Tagore and Xu Zhimo through China on their landmark tour. In 1925 Elmhirst married Dorothy Whitney Straight, an American heiress who brought considerable wealth to their union and had previously funded Elmhirst's position at Sriniketan. That same year the Elmhirsts purchased the fourteenth-century Dartington Estate in

The Great Hall at Dartington was built between 1388 and 1400.

Devon, originally constructed for John Holland, Earl of Huntingdon and half-brother of Richard II. Tagore, who had a fondness for Devon, suggested the location to Elmhirst.

The Elmhirsts channeled their resources into the estate, which was in a state of disrepair, and embarked on what they termed the "Dartington Experiment" or the creation of a society that was "sustaining, just, and enriching." The couple restored the estate buildings and set up numerous projects, among them the Dartington Hall School, Dartington Tweed Mill, Dartington Glass, and Dartington College of the Arts.

Motivated by the same underlying desire for communal self-reliance as Santiniketan, Dartington Hall revived the farming and forestry of the estate, launched weaving, cider-making, and building enterprises, and opened a forward-thinking school. The Elmhirsts set out to promote five different aspects: the arts to nourish the human spirit, environmental and economic sustainability, social justice, enterprise to create revenues for charitable activities, and the place itself to maintain and renew the estate for supporting programs. Eventually, the establishment of Dartington Hall would lead to the creation of hundreds of jobs and many community enterprises.

Dartington Hall quickly became a magnet for creative activity, with philosophers, artists, architects, musicians, and writers visiting from around the world and taking up short residencies, including Tagore (who visited three times), Bertrand Russell, Jacqueline du Pré, Aldous Huxley, Ravi Shankar, and, of course, Xu Zhimo.

Xu took great inspiration from both Tagore's Santiniketan and the Elmhirsts' Dartington Hall, so much so that he proposed to establish a similar utopian, cooperative society in China and began looking for locations for such a school in Zhejiang and Jiangsu, both provinces near Shanghai. Elmhirst purportedly offered funding for the project, though Xu's plans never quite took flight.

Birch, Cyril. *Anthology of Chinese Literature: Volume II: From the Fourteenth Century to the Present Day* New York: Grove Press, 1972.

Chai Cao 柴草. *Yidai cainu, kuangshi jiaren: Tushuo Lu Xiaoman* 一代才女, 曠世佳人: 圖說陸小曼 *(A Talented Woman for the Generation, an Incomparable Beauty: Illustrated History of Lu Xiaoman).* Harbin: Harbin chubanshe 哈爾濱出版社, 2004.

Shu Ling'e 舒玲娥, ed. *Yunyou: Pengyou xinzhong de Xu Zhimo* 雲遊: 朋友心中的徐志摩 *(Cloud Wandering: Xu Zhimo in Friends' Minds).* Wuhan: Changjiang wenyi chubanshe 長江文藝出版社, 2005.

Chang, Pang-Mei Natasha. *Bound Feet & Western Dress: A Memoir.* New York: Doubleday-Bantam Press, 1996.

Chen Congzhou 陳從周. *Xu Zhimo nianpu* 徐志摩年譜 *(The Chronology of Xu Zhimo).* 1949. Rpt. Shanghai: Shanghai Shudian 上海書店 (Shanghai Bookstore), 1981.

Denton, Kirk A., and Michael Hockx, eds. *Literary Societies of Republican China.* Lanham, MD: Rowman & Littlefield Publishers, 2008.

Dickinson, Goldsworthy Lowes. *The Autobiography of G. Lowes Dickinson and Other Unpublished Writings.* Edited by Dennis Proctor. London: Duckworth, 1973.

Fairbank, Wilma. *Liang and Lin: Partners in Exploring China's Architectural Past.* Philadelphia: University of Pennsylvania Press, 1994.

Forster, E. M., and Ronald Edmund Balfour. *Goldsworthy Lowes Dickinson.* New York: Harcourt Brace Jovanovich, 1934.

Han Shishan 韓石山. *Xu Zhimo zhuan* 徐志摩傳 *(Biography of Xu Zhimo).* Beijing: Renmin wenxue chubanshe 人民文學出版社, 2014.

Hardy, Florence Emily. *The Life of Thomas Hardy.* London: Studio Editions, 1994.

Hsu, Kai-Yu. *Twentieth Century Chinese Poetry: An Anthology.* Garden City, NY: Doubleday, 1963.

Jiang Fucong 蔣復璁 and Liang Shiqiu 梁實秋, eds. *Xu Zhimo quanji* 徐志摩全集 *(The Collected Works of Xu Zhimo).* Taipei: Zhuanji wenxue chubanshe 傳記文學出版社 (Biographical Literature Publisher) 1969.

Lau, Joseph S. M., and Howard Goldblatt, eds. *The Columbia Anthology of Modern Chinese Literature*. New York: Columbia University Press, 1995.

Laurence, Patricia. *Lily Briscoe's Chinese Eyes: Bloomsbury, Modernism, and China*. Columbia: University of South Carolina Press, 2003.

Lee, Leo Ou-fan. *The Romantic Generation of Modern Chinese Writers*. Cambridge, MA: Harvard University Press, 1973.

Leung, Gaylord Kai-Loh (Liang Xihua 梁錫華). *Hsu Chih-Mo: A Literary Biography*. PhD diss., Hong Kong University and University of London, 1972.

Liang Congjie 梁從誡, ed. *Lin Huiyin wenji* 林徽音文集 (*Collected Works of Lin Huiyin*). Taipei: Tianxia wenhua chuban gongsi 天下文化出版公司 (Commonwealth Publishing Co., Ltd.), 2000.

Liang Shiqiu. *Tan Xu Zhimo* 談徐志摩 (*Talking About Xu Zhimo*). Taipei: Yuandong tushu gongsi 遠東圖書公司 (The Far East Book Company), 1958.

Liang Xihua 梁錫華. *Xu Zhimo xinzhuan* 徐志摩新傳 (*New Biography of Xu Zhimo*). Taipei: Lianjing chuban gongsi 聯經出版公司 (Linking Publishing Company), 1979.

Lin, Julia C. *Modern Chinese Poetry: An Introduction*. Seattle: University of Washington Press, 1972.

Lin Zhu 林洙. *Liang Sicheng, Lin Huiyin yu wo* 梁思成, 林徽因與我 (Liang Sicheng, Lin Huiyin and I). Beijing: Zhongguo qingnian chubanshe 中國青年出版社 (China Youth Publishing Group), 2011.

Lu Yaodong 陸耀東. *Xu Zhimo pingzhuan* 徐志摩評傳 (*Biography of Xu Zhimo*). Taiyuan: Shaanxi renmin chubanshe 陝西人民出版社 (Shaanxi People's Publishing House), 1986.

Monk, Ray. *Bertrand Russell: The Spirit of Solitude, 1872–1921*. New York: Free Press, 1996.

Payne, Robert. *Contemporary Chinese Poetry*. London: George Routledge & Sons, 1947.

Russell, Bertrand. *The Autobiography of Bertrand Russell, 1914–1944*. Boston: Atlantic-Little, Brown, 1951.

Shao Huaqiang 邵華強, ed. *Xu Zhimo yanjiu ziliao* 徐志摩研究資料 (*Research Materials About Xu Zhimo*). Beijing: Zhishi chanquan chubanshe 知識產權出版社, 2011.

Shau Wing Chan. *The Poems of Hsu Chih-Mo*. Poems translated from Chinese with a biographical account, unpublished manuscript.

Singh, Udaya Narayana, and Navdeep Suri, eds. *Rabindranath Tagore: A Commemorative Volume*. New Delhi: Public Diplomacy Div., Ministry of External Affairs, Government of India, 2011.

Song Binghui 宋炳輝. *Xinyue xia de yeying: Xu Zhimo zhuan* 新月下的夜鶯: 徐志摩傳 *(Nightingale Under the Crescent Moon: Biography of Xu Zhimo)*. Shanghai: Shanghai weni chubanshe 上海文藝出版社 (Shanghai Literature Publisher), 1993. Rpt. Shanghai: Fudan daxue chubanshe 復旦大學出版社 (Fudan University Publisher), 2010.

Song, Binghui 宋炳輝. *Xu Zhimo riji de faxian ji qi jiazhi* 徐志摩日記的發現及其價值 *(The Finding of Xu Zhimo's Diaries and Their Values)*. Webhui dushu zhoubao 文匯讀書周報 (Wenhui Book Review), April 26, 2002.

Spalding, Francis. *The Bloomsbury Group*. London: National Portrait Gallery, 2005.

Spence, Jonathan D. *The Gate of Heavenly Peace: The Chinese and Their Revolution, 1895–1980*. New York: Viking Press, 1981.

Spence, Jonathan D., and Annping Chin. *The Chinese Century: A Photographic History of the Last Hundred Years*. New York: Random House, 1996.

Tan Chung et al. *Tagore and China*. New York: Sage Publications, 2011.

Welland, Sasha Su-Ling. *Thousand Miles of Dreams: The Journeys of Two Chinese Sisters*. Lanham, MD: Rowman & Littlefield Publishers, 2006.

Wilkinson, L. P. *A Century of King's, 1873–1972*. Cambridge: Kings College, 1980.

Wilkinson, L. P. *Kingsmen of a Century, 1873–1972*. Cambridge: King's College, 1980.

Xiao Qian (Hsiao Ch'ien) 蕭乾. *A Harp with a Thousand Strings*. London: Pilot Press, 1944.

Ye, Weili. *Seeing Modernity in China's Name: Chinese Students in the United States, 1900-1927*. Stanford: Stanford University Press, 2001.

Yeh, Michelle. *Anthology of Modern Chinese Poetry*. New Haven: Yale University Press, 1992.

Yeh, Michelle. *Modern Chinese Poetry: Theory and Practice Since 1917*. New Haven: Yale University Press, 1991.

Young, Michael. *Elmhirsts of Dartington: The Creation of a Utopian Community*. Dartington: Dartington Hall Trust, 1996.

Zhu Jihua 朱紀華. *Rabindranath Tagore in Shanghai*. Shanghai: Shanghai Municipal Archives and Consulate General of India, 2012.

Logo for the Crescent Moon Bookstore, 1927.

Student

Consular No. *190/1918*

FORM OF CHINESE CERTIFICATE

In compliance with the provisions of Section 6 of an Act of the Congress of the United States of America, approved July 5, 1884, entitled "An Act to amend an act entitled 'An Act to execute certain treaty stipulations relating to Chinese, approved May 6, 1882.'"

THIS CERTIFICATE is issued by the undersigned, who has been designated for that purpose by the Government of China, to show that the person named hereinafter is a member of one of the exempt classes described in said Act and as such has the permission of said Government to go to and reside within the territory of the United States, after an investigation and verification of the statements contained herein by the lawfully constituted agent of the United States in this country.

The following description is submitted for the identification of the person to whom the certificate relates:—

Application no 202

Name in full, in proper signature of bearer: Hsü Chang-hsü

Title or official rank, if any: --

Physical peculiarities: Group of scars right side of forehead and mole back of neck.

Date of birth: January 5, 1898.

Height: 5 feet 7-1/2 inches

Former occupation: Student

When pursued: 1916-1917

Where pursued: Tientsin (Pei Yang University)

How long pursued: 1 year

Present occupation: Student

When pursued: 1917-1918

Where pursued: Peking (Law School of Government Univ.)

How long pursued: 1 year

Last place of actual residence: Yah Zeh, Chekiang, China.

NOTE.—If a merchant the following blanks should be filled out:

Title of present mercantile business: --

Location of said mercantile business: --

How long said business has been pursued: --

Amount invested (gold) in said business: --

Present estimated value of said business: --

Specific character of merchandise handled in said business: --

NOTE.—If bearer is a traveller the following blanks should be filled out:

Financial standing of bearer in his own country: --

Probable duration of his stay in the United states:

Issued as Shanghai, China, on this 9th day of August 1918

(Signature of Chinese Official.)

(VISE:)
I, the undersigned duly authorized consular officer of the American Government for the territory within which the person named in the above certificate resides, have made a through investigation of the statements contained in the foregoing certificate and have found them to be in all respects true, and accordingly attach my signature and official seal in order that the bearer may be admitted to the United States upon identification as the person represented by the attached photograph, over which I have partly placed my Official seal.

Nelson Trusler Johnson

Consul General of the United States of America. in charge

AUG - 9 1918

$1 AMERICAN CONSULAR SERVICE FEE STAMP

FEE No. 5211

I relied on the translation work of many scholars for the excerpts of Xu Zhimo's writings that appear throughout *Chasing the Modern*.

To start, I would like to express deep gratitude to Shau Wing Chan, professor emeritus of Chinese and Chinese literature in the Department of Asian Languages in the School of Humanities and Sciences, Stanford University, who kindly invited me to draw from his unpublished work, *The Poems of Hsu Chih-mo*. Excerpts of his skillful translations appear throughout *Chasing the Modern*.

I would also like to sincerely thank and give credit to all the scholars and academics whose work I reference throughout the book. Translation credits are as follows.

MAIN MANUSCRIPT

Page XV: Xu Zhimo, "A Chance Encounter," translated by Michelle Yeh, in *Anthology of Modern Chinese Poetry* (Yale University Press, 1992). Original source: *The Collected Works of Xu Zhimo (Xu Zhimo quanji* 徐志摩全集), by Jiang Fucong 蔣復璁 and Liang Shiqiu 梁實秋.

Page 3: Poetry excerpt from Xu Zhimo, "A Second Farewell to Cambridge," translated by Kai-Yu Hsu, *Twentieth Century Chinese Poetry: An Anthology* (Doubleday, 1963). Original Source: *Crescent Moon Monthly*, Vol. 1, No. 10.

Pages 16-17: Excerpt from Xu Zhimo, "Contemplations of My Journey to America," in *The Gate of Heavenly Peace: The Chinese and Their Revolution*, by Jonathan D. Spence (Viking Press, 1981). Original source: *The Collected Works of Xu Zhimo.*

Page 20: Excerpt from Xu Zhimo, "Contemplations of My Journey to America," in *The Gate of Heavenly Peace: The Chinese and Their Revolution*, by Jonathan D. Spence (Viking Press, 1981). Original source: *The Collected Works of Xu Zhimo.*

Xu's 1918 immigration visa that allowed him to study in the United States.

Page 30: Poem excerpt from Xu Zhimo, "The Dewdrops on the Grass," translated by Shau Wing Chan, in *The Poems of Hsu Chih-mo* (unpublished manuscript). Original source: *The Collected Works of Xu Zhimo*.

Pages 30-31: Excerpt from Xu Zhimo, *Fierce Tiger*, translated by Shau Wing Chan, in *The Poems of Hsu Chih-mo* (unpublished manuscript). Original source: *The Collected Works of Xu Zhimo*.

Page 35: Excerpt from Xu Zhimo, letter to Zhang Youyi requesting a divorce, translated by Shau Wing Chan, in *The Poems of Hsu Chih-mo* (unpublished manuscript). Original source: *The Collected Works of Xu Zhimo*.

Page 37: Excerpt from Xu Zhimo, "The Cambridge I Knew," translated by Cyril Birch, in *Anthology of Chinese Literature, Volume II: From the Fourteenth Century to the Present Day*, edited by Cyril Birch (Grove Press, 1972). Original source: *The Collected Works of Xu Zhimo*.

Page 39: Poem from Xu Zhimo, "To Mansfield: A Lament," translated by Shau Wing Chan, in *The Poems of Hsu Chih-mo* (unpublished manuscript). Original source: *Collected Works of Xu Zhimo*.

Page 44: First excerpt from Liang Qichao's letter to Xu Zhimo, translated by Shau Wing Chan, in *The Poems of Hsu Chih-mo* (unpublished manuscript). Original source: *The Collected Works of Xu Zhimo*.

Page 44: Second excerpt from Liang Qichao's letter to Xu Zhimo, in *The Gate of Heavenly Peace: The Chinese and Their Revolution*, by Jonathan D. Spence (Viking Press, 1981). Original source: *The Collected Works of Xu Zhimo*.

Page 45: Excerpt from Xu Zhimo's letter to Liang Qichao, translated by Shau Wing Chan, in *The Poems of Hsu Chih-mo* (unpublished manuscript). Original source: *The Collected Works of Xu Zhimo*.

Pages 45-46: Poetry excerpt from Xu Zhimo, "Sad Thoughts," translated by Shau Wing Chan, in *The Poems of Hsu Chih-mo* (unpublished manuscript). Original source: *The Collected Works of Xu Zhimo*.

Page 49: Poetry excerpt from Rabindranath Tagore, translated by Tan Chun, in *Tagore and China* (SAGE Publications, 2011). Original source: Wilma Cannon Fairbank conveyed this poem from a discussion with her Chinese friends.

Page 50: Excerpt from Xu Zhimo, from a speech given about Tagore, translated by Gaylord Leung, in *Hsu Chih-Mo: A Literary Biography*. Original source: *The Collected Works of Xu Zhimo*.

Page 58: Both excerpts from Xu Zhimo's letter to Lu Xiaoman, translated by Shau Wing Chan, in *The Poems of Hsu Chih-mo* (unpublished manuscript). Original source: *The Collected Works of Xu Zhimo*.

Pages 61-62: Excerpt from Xu Zhimo, a memorial essay for son Peter, in *Bound Feet & Western Dress*, by Pang-Mei Natasha Chang (Doubleday, 1996). Original source: *The Collected Works of Xu Zhimo.*

Pages 71-72: Excerpt from Lu Xiaoman's letter to Xu Zhimo, translated by Shau Wing Chan, in *The Poems of Hsu Chih-mo* (unpublished manuscript). Original source: *The Collected Works of Xu Zhimo.*

Page 74: Text quoted from Liang Qichao's speech, given at Xu Zhimo and Lu Xiaoman's wedding, translated by Shau Wing Chan, in *The Poems of Hsu Chih-mo* (unpublished manuscript). Original source: *The Collected Works of Xu Zhimo.*

Page 74: Excerpt from Liang Qichao's letter to his daughter, in *The Gate of Heavenly Peace: The Chinese and Their Revolution*, by Jonathan D. Spence (Viking Press, 1981). Original Source: Liang Qichao, *Nianpu.*

Page 76: Excerpt from Xu Zhimo's journal, translated by Gaylord Leung, in *Hsu Chih-Mo: A Literary Biography.* Original source: *The Collected Works of Xu Zhimo.*

Page 76: Text quoted from Xu Zhimo's letter to Leonard Elmhirst, from the Dartington Hall Trust Archives.

Page 77: Excerpt from Xu Zhimo's letter to Lu Xiaoman, translated by Gaylord Leung, in *Hsu Chih-Mo: A Literary Biography* (Hong Kong University and University of London, 1972). Original source: *The Collected Works of Xu Zhimo.*

Page 79: First excerpt from Xu Zhimo's journal, translated by Shau Wing Chan, in *The Poems of Hsu Chih-mo* (unpublished manuscript). Original source: *The Collected Works of Xu Zhimo.*

Page 79: Poetry excerpted from Xu Zhimo, "The Last Days of Spring," translated by Shau Wing Chan, in *The Poems of Hsu Chih-mo* (unpublished manuscript). Original source: *The Collected Works of Xu Zhimo.*

Page 81: Excerpt from Xu Zhimo, editorial letter in the *Morning Post Literary Supplement (Chenbao)*, translated by Shau Wing Chan, in *The Poems of Hsu Chih-mo* (unpublished manuscript). Original source: *The Collected Works of Xu Zhimo.*

Page 82: Excerpt from Xu Zhimo, editorial letter in *Shikan Poetry Monthly*, translated by Shau Wing Chan, in *The Poems of Hsu Chih-mo* (unpublished manuscript). Original source: *The Collected Works of Xu Zhimo.*

Page 83: Excerpt from Xu Zhimo, preface to *A Night in Florence*, translated by Shau Wing Chan, in *The Poems of Hsu Chih-mo* (unpublished manuscript). Original source: *The Collected Works of Xu Zhimo.*

Page 85: Excerpt from Xu Zhimo, article in *Crescent Moon Monthly*, translated by Shau Wing Chan, in *The Poems of Hsu Chih-mo* (unpublished manuscript). Original source: *The Collected Works of Xu Zhimo*.

Page 86: Poetry excerpt from Xu Zhimo, "Life," translated by Shau Wing Chan, in *The Poems of Hsu Chih-mo* (unpublished manuscript). Original source: *The Collected Works of Xu Zhimo*.

Page 90: Poetry excerpt from Xu Zhimo, "Love's Inspiration," translated by Shau Wing Chan, in *The Poems of Hsu Chih-mo* (unpublished manuscript). Original source: *The Collected Works of Xu Zhimo*.

Page 93: Poetry excerpt from Xu Zhimo, "You Are Going," translated by Shau Wing Chan, in *The Poems of Hsu Chih-mo* (unpublished manuscript). Original source: *The Collected Works of Xu Zhimo*.

Page 96: Excerpt from Xu Zhimo, "Wanting to Fly," translated by Leo Ou-fan Lee, in *The Romantic Generation of Modern Chinese Writers* (Harvard University Press, 1973). Original source: *The Collected Works of Xu Zhimo*.

Page 97: Poetry excerpt from Xu Zhimo, "Love's Inspiration," translated by Shau Wing Chan, in *The Poems of Hsu Chih-mo* (unpublished manuscript). Original source: *The Collected Works of Xu Zhimo*.

SELECTED WORKS BY XU ZHIMO

Pages 122-123: "On Hearing the Chant of Intercession at the Temple of Heaven's Stillness at Ch'angchou," translated by Cyril Birch, from *Anthology of Chinese Literature: Volume II: From the Fourteenth Century to the Present Day*, edited by Cyril Birch (Grove Press, 1972).

Pages 124-125: "Seven, Stone Tiger Lane," translated by Cyril Birch, in *Anthology of Chinese Literature: Volume II: From the Fourteenth Century to the Present Day*, edited by Cyril Birch (Grove Press, 1972).

Page 126: "In Search of a Bright Star," translated by Julia C. Lin, in *Modern Chinese Poetry: An Introduction* by Julia C. Lin (University of Washington Press, 1973).

Page 127: "Joy of the Snowflake," translated by Cyril Birch, in *Anthology of Chinese Literature: Volume II: From the Fourteenth Century to the Present Day*, edited by Cyril Birch (Grove Press, 1972).

Pages 128-129: "A Night in Florence," translated by Kai-Yu Hsu, in *Twentieth Century Chinese Poetry: An Anthology* by Kai-Yu Hsu (Doubleday, 1963).

Pages 130-131: "Sea Rhyme," translated by Cyril Birch, in *Anthology of Chinese Literature: Volume II: From the Fourteenth Century to the Present Day*, edited by Cyril Birch (Grove Press, 1972).

Page 132: "What Exactly Is This Thing Called Love?" translated by Kai-Yu Hsu, in *Twentieth Century Chinese Poetry: An Anthology* by Kai-Yu Hsu (Doubleday, 1963).

Page 133: "I Have One Love," translated by Julia C. Lin, in *Modern Chinese Poetry: An Introduction* by Julia C. Lin (University of Washington Press, 1973).

Page 134: "Follow Me," translated by Yuan K'o-chia, in *Contemporary Chinese Poetry*, edited by Robert Payne (Routledge, 1947).

Page 135: "A P'i-pa Tune in an Alley at Midnight," translated by Kai-yu Hsu, in *Twentieth Century Chinese Poetry: An Anthology* by Kai-Yu Hsu (Doubleday, 1963).

Page 136: "A Second Farewell to Cambridge," translated by Kai-Yu Hsu, in *Twentieth Century Chinese Poetry: An Anthology* by Kai-Yu Hsu (Doubleday, 1963).

Page 137: "I Know Not in Which Way the Wind Blows," translated by Shau Wing Chan, in *The Poetry of Hsu Chih-mo* by Shau Wing Chan (unpublished manuscript).

Pages 138-139: "Thomas Hardy," translated by Michelle Yeh, in *Anthology of Modern Chinese Poetry* by Michelle Yeh (Yale University Press, 1992).

Page 140: "Birth of Spring," translated by Julia C. Lin, in *Modern Chinese Poetry: An Introduction* by Julia C. Lin (University of Washington Press, 1973).

Page 141: "Roaming in the Clouds," translated by Julia C. Lin, in *Modern Chinese Poetry: An Introduction* by Julia C. Lin (University of Washington Press, 1973).

Page 142: "On the Bus," translated by Michelle Yeh, in *Anthology of Modern Chinese Poetry* by Michelle Yeh (Yale University Press, 1992).

Pages 145-150: "The Cambridge I Knew," translated by Cyril Birch, in *Anthology of Chinese Literature: Volume II: From the Fourteenth Century to the Present Day*, edited by Cyril Birch (Grove Press, 1972).

ILLUSTRATION CREDITS

Pages VI, VII, X, XVI, 2, 6, 9, 14, 27, 34, 60, 65, 67, 70, 80, 88, 98, 102, 120, 153, 178, 184, 191, 192 — Hsu Family Archives

Page 11 — *Who's Who in China* 3rd ed, *The China Weekly Review* (Shanghai), 1925, p.497

Pages 21, 47 — From *Collected Works of Lin Huiyin*, edited by Liang Congjie

Page 23 — By Ottoline Morrell (1873-1938) via Wikimedia Commons

Pages 24, 112 — By Sue Martin, courtesy of Hsu Family Archives

Page 33 — By Peter Savary, via *Goldsworthy Lowes Dickinson* by E.M. Forster (Harcourt Brace Jovanovich, 1973)

Page 42 — Courtesy of Ken Mayer

Page 52 — Courtesy of Narayana Udaya Singh and Navdeep Suri

Page 54, 83, 121, 181 — Public Domain

Page 94 — By Art Ramierz, courtesy of Hsu Family Archives

Page 108 — Courtesy of Martin Ingram

Page 144 — By Zhao Jiancheng

Page 179 — By Lou Jian Jun

Page 180 — Chen Family Archives

Page 188 — From *Seeking Modernity in China's Name: Chinese Students in the United States, 1900 – 1927* by Weili Ye

Page 193 — Dartington Hall Archives

ACKNOWLEDGMENTS

To write *Chasing the Modern* I went on many literary adventures over the past few years, traveling to dozens of cities on three different continents and one subcontinent to research and report.

But it wasn't as if every occasion brought me to a meticulously organized archival library, a professor's book-lined office, or a charming teahouse. On the contrary, my sleuthing took me to places as disparate as a desolate mountainside in northern China, a blazing marketplace in Kolkata, and the Cambridge countryside, where I sped on an out-of-control bicycle one late night until I crashed into a bush. While I might have made most of these travels on my own, so many of you took this journey with me, and indeed were instrumental in sending me down the right paths.

I owe gratitude to so many people, most of whom I will endeavor to name here.

To my sisters, Angela King, Fern Tse, Margaret Mow, the greatest collaborators in legacy and life I could ask for. Your knowledge and insight have been invaluable to me. Each of you has had a tremendous passion for understanding our grandfather. Thank you for sharing this deep interest in our family history.

Heartfelt thanks to my wife, Lily Pao Hsu, and daughter, Alle Hsu, who have offered me their unwavering support and often their good company during my research travels. Alle also showed an extraordinary curiosity in her great-grandfather, which in part has sustained my ongoing interest.

I relied heavily on personal interviews with and material written by the following scholars: Professor Emeritus Alan Donald James MacFarlane, my friend and guide to all things Cambridge and English: your foreword to this book reflects your humor, effusiveness, and shining intelligence. Professor Michelle

Yeh: your essay, "Xu Zhimo: The Quintessential Modern Poet," brings laudable insight to his poetry. Dr. Gaylord Kai-Loh Leung, for our long conversations by telephone, fax, and post. Professor Shau Wing Chan, whose academic writings about Xu provided an invaluable overview of the poet's life and work. Professor Cyril Birch, who was the first person to stimulate my interest in my grandfather's work. Professor Leo Ou-fan Lee, one of the leading scholars of romantic Chinese literature, whose scholarly work greatly informed me. Chen Congzhou, who wrote *The Chronology of Xu Zhimo* and whom I met in Shanghai shortly after he had suffered a stroke. Chen worked devotedly to preserve Xu's legacy. Without his efforts, many of Xu's writings would have been lost. To all of you I say a heartfelt thank you. Without your outstanding work and deep knowledge of Xu Zhimo's history and poems and essays, *Chasing the Modern* would not have been possible.

Writing about a person who lived two generations removed, from a period of history and from a place radically different from my own experience posed a significant challenge for me. Alison Singh Gee, *Chasing the Modern*'s editor, helped me navigate through this process. The result, I hope, is a narrative that the reader finds to be lyrical, nuanced, and empathetic. Alison's creativity and dedication helped me tremendously as I worked to capture the extraordinary life of my grandfather, a story that I hope adds to his legacy.

To Katie Salisbury, much gratitude for your meticulous and inspired work on this book's chronology, glossary, and photo rights. Your talents and commitment shine through on every page of *Chasing the Modern*.

Chia-ying Shih, I am grateful for your tireless efforts to help with the Chinese-language research of Xu Zhimo's writings and other supporting material.

To Pang-Mei Natasha Chang, author of the groundbreaking memoir *Bound Feet & Western Dress*, my grandmother Zhang Youyi's memoir: your research gave us an intimate portrait of my grandparents' marriage set against a fascinating early twentieth-century landscape. *Chasing the Modern* owes much to your meticulous work to record Zhang Youyi's extraordinary life.

Henrietta Lo, a highly respected reference librarian at California State University in Chico, was instrumental in helping the Hsu family with critical research on Xu Zhimo's writings over the course of many years. Fueled by a deep personal interest in the poet, Ms. Lo spent many hours with us, discussing her research and bringing to our attention new articles and commentary about our grandfather.

To the knowledgeable librarians who guided me through their archives: thank you, Wang Zhengzhi and Jim Cheng of C. V. Starr East Asian Library, Columbia University, and Shen Zhijia of the East Asia Library, University of Washington.

Thank you to researchers Ron Wells in Newport Beach, Alexandra Saunders in Cambridge, and Bruce Milner, dedicated archivist in Sawston, England.

Additionally, I would like to thank the following people at Rabindra Bhavana, Visva Bharati, Santiniketan, India: Professor Sushanta Datta Gupta, vice chancellor, Professor Udaya Narayana Singh, pro-vice chancellor, and Professor Avijit Banerjee, Chinese Studies.

To Chin-Yee Lai, whose superb eye and talent as a book designer brought this book to life, and to her partner Simon Lee, for managing this project. Thank you to layout artists Candace Kita and Jackson Lin—you each offered something unique to this book.

My gratitude goes to Pan Qian, curator of the Xu Zhimo Residence Museum in Xiashi, China; Yvonne Widger, the archivist at Dartington Hall, Devon, U.K.; Fordyce Williams of Clark University Archives Office; and the Modern Archives at King's College, Cambridge University.

Thank you for your translation help, Miranda Jiang, Hongni Chu, Ching Chu, Chris Tu, May Hsu, and Al Chen.

And, in no particular order, many thanks to the following for support throughout:

Jeff Sims and Jennifer Lee Sims, Patricia Laurence, Xiao Ying Chinnery, Dr. Ho Yong, Ben Wang, Dr. Zilan Wang, Lou Jian Jun, Sue J. Martin, Chou Yi-an, Chang Ping Fan, Ken Mayer, Martin Ingram, Sarah MacFarlane, Chen Shengwu, Dr. Yue Ouyang, Le Fong, Lou Shuai, Xiuhong Shen, Yunpeng Zhang, Yang Liju, Christopher Burkhardt, Jean Hastings Ardell, Zhao Jiancheng, Lee Lin, Art Ramirez, Professor Tan Chung, Professor Fu Guangming, Professor Kui Yu-Zhang, Judy Baba, Professor Ako Kato, Yang Lian, Nicholas Chrimes, Ya Hsien, Mark Hebner, India Cooper, Nancy Williams, Ajay Singh, Professor Peter Xiao, Chin Moon Fun, Xu Guohua, Zhou Tinghua, Liu Yanqi, Yue Zhengyang, Chen Xin, Liao Yen-po, Akiko Mikumo, Shao Huaqiang, Xu Xiheng, Cristina Klenz and Professor Hiro Kato.

Photo by Cristina Salvador Klenz

TONY S. HSU was born in Shanghai shortly after the end of World War II. As a toddler, Hsu and his sisters were raised by his grandmother, Zhang Youyi, while his parents pursued their studies in America. In the late 1940s, Zhang and her young charges left China amidst national political turmoil and settled in Hong Kong. At age six, Hsu and his sisters emigrated to New York to join their parents and began a new life in America. Hsu ultimately received his BS in Electrical Engineering from University of Michigan and a Ph.D in Applied Physics from Yale University. He has been an executive for several technology companies. Hsu lives with his fashion designer wife, Lily Pao Hsu, and his filmmaker daughter, Alexandra, in Southern California. *Chasing the Modern* is his first book.